CONTENTS

CUISINART AIR FRYER TOASTER OVEN 7

What Is the Cuisinart AirFryer Toaster Oven? 7

Specifications of The CuisinArt AirFryer Toaster Oven 8

The Benefits of The CuisinArt Toaster Oven... 9

General Cooking Tips and Tricks When Using CuisinArt AirFryer Toaster...... 10

Recommended Cooking Times, Temperatures, And Portions 13

Cleaning Tips 14

CuisinArt AirFryer Toaster Oven FAQs 15

BREAKFAST RECIPES 16

Coconut Pineapple Oatmeal 16

Breakfast Egg Muffins 17

Healthy Egg Bake 18

Vegan Baked Oatmeal... 19

Easy Banana Bread 20

Baked Omelet... 21

Sausage Veggie Egg Bake 22

Baked Donuts... 23

Healthy Broccoli Muffins 24

Easy Crust-less Quiche 25

Cheese Frittata... 26

Healthy Breakfast Egg Casserole 27

Delicious Berry Oatmeal 28

Italian Frittata.. 29

Herb Egg Muffins 30

POULTRY RECIPES **31**

Greek Chicken.. 31

Juicy Chicken Breast.. 32

Baked Chicken Breasts 33

Flavors Chicken Thighs 34

Cheesy Parmesan Chicken 35

Curried Chicken... 36

BBQ Chicken Wings 37

Turkey Tenderloin... 38

Chicken Meatballs 39

Pesto Chicken.. 40

Lemon Pepper Chicken 41

Meatballs 42

Delicious Chicken Wings... 43

Chili Garlic Chicken Wings 44

Tasty Fajita Chicken.. 45

Delicious Chicken Tenders 46

Meatballs 47

Turkey Meatballs... 48

Herb Chicken Wings 49

Parmesan Chicken Nuggets 50

Sweet & Spicy Chicken Wings 51

Tasty Chicken Fritters 52

Rosemary Chicken 53

Delicious Turkey Burgers 54

Easy Cajun Chicken.. 55

SEAFOOD RECIPES **56**

Delicious Cajun Salmon 56

Flavors Lemon Cod 57

Spicy Tilapia 58

Crab Cakes 59

Garlic Lime Shrimp.. 60

Dijon Salmon 61

Tasty Shrimp Fajitas 62

Parmesan Walnut Salmon 63

Greek Pesto Salmon 64

Easy Baked Tilapia 65

Cajun Catfish Fillets... 66

Blackened Mahi Mahi 67

Salmon Patties 69

Crab Cakes... 70

Salmon Dill Patties.. 71

Spicy Shrimp.. 72

Air Fried White Fish Fillet 73

Coconut Shrimp... 74

Parmesan Fish Fillets 76

Shrimp Fajitas 77

Chipotle Shrimp 78

Air Fried Crab Cakes 79

Garlic Butter Shrimp 80

Tasty Shrimp Fajitas 81

Herb Salmon 82

SNACKS & APPETIZERS **83**

Potato Wedges 83

Tasty Ranch Potatoes 85

Spicy Cheese Dip 86

Zucchini Patties 87

Sweet Potato Fries.. 88

Cinnamon Maple Chickpeas 89

Spicy Chickpeas 90

Parmesan Brussels sprouts 91

Crispy Cauliflower Florets... 92

Air Fried Walnuts.. 93

Jalapeno Poppers 94

Spicy Cauliflower Florets 95

Baked Cheese Dip.. 96

Onion Dip 97

Delicious Ricotta Dip.. 98

Garlic Cheese Dip 99

Spinach Dip.. 100

Spicy Almonds 101

Spicy Brussels sprouts 102

Herb Mushrooms 103

DESSERTS **104**

Banana Butter Brownie 104

Apple Bars 105

Butter Cake 106

Cinnamon Cranberry Muffins 107

Delicious Apple Cake 108

Apple Crisp 109

Easy Mini Chocolate Cake 111

Almond Raspberry Muffins 112

Tasty Baked Apples 113

Cinnamon Baked Peaches 114

Healthy Carrot Cake 115

Cinnamon Carrot Muffins 116

Tasty Lemon Cupcakes 117

Brownie Muffins 118

Delicious Scalloped Pineapple 119

CUISINART AIR FRYER TOASTER OVEN

The emergence of many lifestyle diseases such as diabetes, high blood pressure, and obesity has pushed many people in the country to embrace healthy eating habits. Healthy eating habits do not only entail the consumption of organic produce but also cooking with less oil. This is the reason why there are so many kitchen appliances available in the market that allows foodies like you to be able to cook food in healthy ways. And while there are many kitchen appliances that you can use to make healthier foods, what makes the Cuisine Air Fryer Toaster Oven better than its counterparts? Read on and find out why!

What Is the Cuisinart AirFryer Toaster Oven?

The Cuisinart AirFryer Toaster Oven is the newest addition to the line of innovative kitchen appliances of CuisinArt. As the name implies, it is an air fryer but can also be extended as a toaster and an oven. With this kitchen appliance, you get three functions in one machine. How is that for convenience?

This innovative kitchen workhorse is a full-size toaster oven that has a built-in air fryer. With these many functions, not only can you fry healthily using this kitchen appliance, but you can also broil, toast, bake, and cook just about anything your heart desired.

It achieves all of these by using a powerful hot air technology that allows you to cook your favorite fried goodies without the need for oil. And since it is technically a toaster oven, it is small enough to fit on your countertop.

Specifications of The CuisinArt AirFryer Toaster Oven

The CuisinArt Toaster Oven is an innovative take of your generic toaster oven as you can extend its use from a simple air fryer to an oven and toaster. Below are the specifications of the CuisinArt AirFryer Toaster Oven.

- **Power Light Indicator:** The power light will turn on and remain lit when the oven is in use. This is to let anyone know that the surface of the oven is hot.

- **On/Oven Timer Dial:** Use this dial to set the desired cooking time for your food. The timer ranges from 1 minute to an hour. This dial does not work for the Toast Setting.

- **Oven Temperature Dial:** This feature allows you to set the desired temperature when cooking your food. The temperature range is from less than 150oF to 450oF.

- **Function Dial:** This particular dial allows you to select the desired cooking method. Choose from Warm, Broil, Toast, Bake, Convection Broil, Convection Bake, and Air Fry.

- **On/Toast Timer Dial:** This dial allows you to choose the desired toast shade from light to dark. To use this dial, choose Toast on your Function Dial first then select the setting for your toast dial.

- **Light Button:** This button allows you to turn on the interior oven light while the oven door is closed. This allows you to see how your food looks like while cooking without opening the oven door. Not opening the oven door is ideal when cooking so that you conserve the temperature inside your hot oven.

- **Safety Auto-Off Door Switch:** This toaster oven comes with the Safety Auto-Off switch that cuts off the power when the oven door is opened.

- **Pull-Out Crumb Tray:** The crumb tray is positioned at the bottom of the toaster oven for easy cleanup. All there is to it is to pull out the crumb tray to remove bits and pieces of food that have fallen at the bottom of the oven during cooking.

- **Baking Pan Drip Tray:** Aside from the crumb tray, it also comes with a drip tray that you can use when roasting food.

- **Cord storage:** The CuisinArt comes with cord storage located at the rear portion of the kitchen appliance so that you can keep your countertop neat and orderly.

The Benefits of The CuisinArt Toaster Oven

The CuisinArt Toaster Oven is unlike any toaster oven or air fryer that you have ever seen before. It comes with so many innovative features that make it stand out from the rest of its competition. Below are the benefits that you will surely enjoy if you get the CuisinArt Toaster Oven:

- **Cook healthier foods:** The main purpose why this kitchen appliance was designed was to encourage people to eat healthier yet delicious foods. You can cook a wide variety of your fried favorites without using too much oil.

- **Seven functions:** The CuisinArt Toaster Oven comes with seven functions. Aside from being an air fryer, you can also use it to convection bake, convection broil, broil, bake, warm, and toast your food.

- **Small frame but large interior:** This 0.6 cubic foot kitchen appliance is small enough to fit on your kitchen counter. This is a space-saving feature that allows you to maximize your kitchen space. Although it has a small body frame, the interior is large enough for you to bake a 12-inch pizza or toast 6 slices of bread, and air fry 3-pound chicken wings.

- **Low power consumption:** The CuisinArt Toaster Oven has a low power consumption of 1800 watts. This is a great kitchen appliance for those who have energy-saving homes.

- **Non-stick easy to clean interior:** The interior of the CuisinArt Toaster Oven is designed to have a non-stick coating. This means that cleaning up its interior is such as breeze and you don't have to worry about soot settling inside the interior.

- **Comes with functional accessories:** To maximize the use of the CuisinArt Toaster Oven, it includes functional accessories such as the oven rack, baking pan, and air fryer basket. All of these accessories can be removed from the oven for easy cleanup.

- **Quiet operation:** Perhaps one of the best features of this kitchen appliance is that it is designed to run on quiet operation. Unlike conventional air fryers that really makes these loud whirring sounds, the CuisinArt Toaster Oven does not produce loud noises so you can maintain the Zen in your kitchen.

General Cooking Tips and Tricks When Using CuisinArt AirFryer Toaster

There are certain things that you need to know when using the CuisinArt AirFryer Toaster. This section will give you the general cooking guidelines so that you can optimize the use of your air fryer toaster oven.

- **Broiling and Convection Broiling:** When using this function, place the AirFryer basket on top of the baking pan. Set the Function Dial to Broil or Convection Broil and turn on the on/Oven Timer Dial to choose the desired cooking time. For best results, do not use glass oven dishes to broil and always keep an eye on your food while cooking to avoid over broiling. Use this function to cook all types of meats. You can also use this function to make casseroles and gratin.

- **Baking and Convection Baking:** When using this function, place the Baking Pan on the Oven Rack. Set the Function Dial to Bake or Convection Bake and turn on the on/Oven Timer Dial to choose the desired cooking time. It is crucial that you preheat the toaster oven for 5 minutes prior to baking custards, cakes, and other pastries. For larger items such as chicken, place the baking pan in rack Position 1 (near the bottom of the oven). On the other hand, there is a big difference when using Baking and Convection Baking (this is also true for Broiling and Convection Broiling). Select Convection Bake if you require even browning on your food. If you are using this setting, make sure that you reduce the temperature by 25°F as the temperature gets evenly distributed inside the oven under this setting.

- **Warm:** Fit the Baking Pan or Oven Rack in Position 2 (one level above Position 1). Set the Temperature Dial and Function Dial to Warm before turning the on/Oven Timer Dial to the desired warming time. Once the timer is off, turn off the toaster oven.

- **Toast:** Fit the Oven Rack in Position 2 then place the items on the rack. If you are going to toast a slice of bread, make sure to place it in the middle of the rack. For more items, make sure that they are evenly spaced. Set the

Function Dial to Toast then the on/Toast Timer Dial to choose the desired color setting of your toast.

- **AirFry:** Place the AirFryer Basket on the Baking Pan in Position 2. Select the AirFry on the Function Dial and set the Temperature Dial to the desired temperature. Tun the On/Oven Timer Dial to set the desired cooking time. When air frying, you can use a little oil but only spritz the surface of your food with oil then massage to distribute the oil evenly. You can also use an assortment of coatings such as corn flakes, potato chips, breadcrumbs, and panko to make your air fried favorites more flavorful. Moreover, it is also important to flip your food halfway through the cooking time for even cooking.

Recommended Cooking Times, Temperatures, And Portions

When cooking with the CuisinArt AirFryer Toaster Oven, it is important that you know proper portioning of your food so that you can make out the most of your cooking time and temperature. Thus, below is a tabulate guide on the recommended cooking times and temperature based on your food types and portions:

Food Types	Recommended Portions	Temperature (ºF)	Time (minutes)
Bacon	8 slices	400	8 to 10 mins
Chicken Wings	20 wings	400	20 to 25 mins
Frozen appetizers (i.e. popcorn, mozzarella sticks)	1 ½ pounds	400	5 to 7 mins
Frozen chicken nuggets	1 pound	400	10 mins
Frozen fish sticks	12 ounces	400	8 mins
Frozen fries	1 to 2 pounds	450	15 to 25 mins
Steak	1 pound	450	15 to 20 mins
Chicken meat	1 pound	450	30 to 35 mins

Cleaning Tips

Cleaning your CuisinArt AirFryer Toaster Oven can increase the lifespan of your kitchen appliance. Below are the things that you need to remember when cleaning this toaster oven air fryer:

- Always allow the oven to completely cool before cleaning. Moreover, unplug the oven from the outlet for safety purposes.

- Do not use any abrasive cleaners such as steel wool pads as they might damage the surface coating of your kitchen appliance. Wipe the exterior with a clean damp cloth and dry thoroughly.

- If you need to apply a cleansing agent such as soap, make sure that you apply it on the damp cloth and not on the toaster's surface. You can do this when cleaning the interior of your kitchen appliance.

- Handwash the accessories in hot soapy water. Use a nylon scouring pad to remove hard-to-remove dirt. Never place them in the dishwasher as they are not designed to be dishwasher safe.

- Clean the crumb tray and drip pan just as you would with the accessories.

- Always clean your oven after every use to maintain its performance.

- Never wrap the cord around the outside of your hot oven. You may use the cord storage cleats at the rear side of your oven to keep the wirings in place.

CuisinArt AirFryer Toaster Oven FAQs

#1: Can I use aluminum foil to cover my food and place it directly on the oven rack?

No. The foil prevents the fat from falling to the Drip Tray and may cause accumulation of grease on the surface, which is a fire hazard. However, if you still wish to use the foil, place the Baking Tray in place then put the foil-covered food. Do not use the oven rack.

#2: What is the maximum amount of food that I can cook in the CuisinArt AirFryer Toaster Oven?

You can only put a maximum of 3 pounds of food at one time. However, make sure that it is not too bulky as oversized foods may touch the heating elements of your food causing it to burn. For a safer method of cooking, slice your food to manageable pieces and evenly distribute them on the baking tray or rack.

#3: How many rack positions does the CuisinArt AirFryer Toaster Oven has?

There are only two rack positions available on the CuisinArt AirFryer Toaster Oven. Position 1 refers to the bottom position where you can place your rack while Position 2 means positioning your rack or tray in the middle of the kitchen appliance. Follow the recommendations of your recipe when selecting which rack position, you should choose when cooking foods.

BREAKFAST RECIPES

Coconut Pineapple Oatmeal

 Time: 50 minutes   🧢 Serve: 6

Nutritional Value

(Amount per Serving):

Calories 304
Fat 16.2 g
Carbohydrates 33.5 g
Sugar 13.1 g
Protein 7.6 g
Cholesterol 85 mg

Ingredients:

- 2 eggs, lightly beaten
- 2 cups old-fashioned oats
- ½ cup unsweetened coconut flakes
- 1 cup pineapple, crushed
- ½ tsp vanilla
- 2/3 cup milk
- 1/3 cup yogurt
- 1/3 cup butter, melted
- ½ tsp baking powder
- 1/3 cup brown sugar
- ½ tsp salt

Directions:

1. Fit the oven with the rack in position 1. Grease 8-inch baking dish and set aside.
2. In a large bowl, mix together oats, baking powder, brown sugar, and salt.
3. In a separate bowl, beat eggs with vanilla, milk, yogurt, and butter.
4. Add egg mixture into the oat mixture and stir to combine. Add coconut and pineapple and stir until well combined.
5. Pour oat mixture into the prepared baking dish.
6. Set to bake at 350 for 40 minutes, after 5 minutes, place the baking dish in the oven.
7. Serve and enjoy.

Breakfast Egg Muffins

 Time: 35 minutes 　 Serve: 6

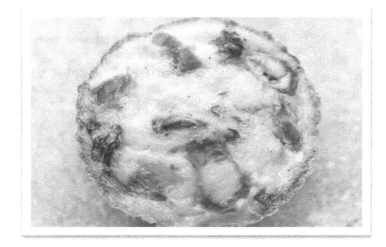

Nutritional Value

(Amount per Serving):

Calories 81
Fat 4.3 g
Carbohydrates 4.8 g
Sugar 3.2 g
Protein 6.3 g
Cholesterol 139 mg

Ingredients:

- 5 eggs

- 1 spring onion, chopped

- ½ cup kale, shredded

- 3 tomatoes, chopped

- 2/3 cup milk

- 1/8 tsp pepper

- ¼ tsp salt

Directions:

1. Fit the oven with the rack in position 1. Grease a 6-hole muffin tin and set aside.
2. In a mixing bowl, whisk eggs with milk, pepper, and salt. Stir in tomatoes, kale, and onion.
3. Pour egg mixture in a prepared muffin tin.
4. Set to bake at 350 for 25 minutes, after 5 minutes, place muffin tin in the oven.
5. Serve and enjoy.

Healthy Egg Bake

 Time: 45 minutes    Serve: 2

Nutritional Value

(Amount per Serving):

Calories 363
Fat 23.9 g
Carbohydrates 8.7 g
Sugar 1.5 g
Protein 28.7 g
Cholesterol 300 mg

Ingredients:

- 3 eggs
- ¼ cup can corn, drained
- 1 ½ tbsp jalapeno, chopped
- ½ cup pepper jack cheese, shredded
- ½ cup cottage cheese
- 1/8 tsp pepper
- 1/8 tsp sea salt

Directions:

1. Fit the oven with the rack in position 1. Grease a 7*5-inch baking dish and set aside.
2. In a bowl, whisk eggs with pepper and salt. Stir in corn, jalapeno, pepper jack cheese, and cottage cheese.
3. Pour egg mixture into prepared dish.
4. Set to bake at 350 for 30 minutes, after 5 minutes, place the baking dish in the oven.
5. Serve and enjoy.

Vegan Baked Oatmeal

 Time: 45 minutes   Serve: 2

Nutritional Value

(Amount per Serving):

Calories 235

Fat 13.2 g

Carbohydrates 28.6 g

Sugar 9.7 g

Protein 4.9 g

Cholesterol 0 mg

Ingredients:

- 1 cup old fashioned rolled oats
- ¼ cup pecan, chopped
- ½ cup unsweetened almond milk
- ¼ tsp baking powder
- ½ tsp vanilla
- ½ tsp ground cinnamon
- 2 tsp olive oil
- 2 tsp maple syrup
- 1 tbsp flax meal
- ¼ cup mashed banana
- Pinch of sea salt

Directions:

1. Fit the oven with the rack in position 1. Grease 7*5-inch baking dish and set aside.
2. In a mixing bowl, add mashed banana, pecan, oats, milk, baking powder, vanilla, cinnamon, olive oil, maple syrup, flaxseed meal, and salt and mix well.
3. Pour mixture into the prepared baking dish.
4. Set to bake at 350 for 35 minutes, after 5 minutes, place the baking dish in the oven.
5. Serve and enjoy.

Easy Banana Bread

 Time: 40 minutes   **Serve: 5**

Nutritional Value

(Amount per Serving):

Calories 129
Fat 3.9 g
Carbohydrates 21.7 g
Sugar 11.3 g
Protein 2.7 g
Cholesterol 33 mg

Ingredients:

- 1 egg
- ¼ tsp ground cinnamon
- ¼ tsp baking soda
- ¼ cup granulated sugar
- ½ cup whole wheat flour
- ¼ tsp vanilla
- 1 tbsp olive oil
- 1 tbsp yogurt
- ¼ cup mashed banana
- 1/8 tsp sea salt

Directions:

1. Fit the oven with the rack in position 1. Grease mini loaf pan and set aside.
2. In a bowl, stir together egg, oil, yogurt, mashed banana, and vanilla. Add flour, cinnamon, baking soda, sugar, and salt and stir until just combined.
3. Pour batter in a prepared loaf pan.
4. Set to bake at 350 for 35 minutes, after 5 minutes, place the loaf pan in the oven.
5. Serve and enjoy.

Baked Omelet

Time: 50 minutes Serve: 6

Nutritional Value

(Amount per Serving):

Calories 200
Fat 12 g
Carbohydrates 6 g
Sugar 3 g
Protein 16 g
Cholesterol 245 mg

Ingredients:

- 8 eggs
- 1 cup milk
- 1/2 cup cheddar cheese, shredded
- 6 oz ham, diced and cooked
- 1 cup bell pepper, chopped
- 1/2 cup onion, chopped
- Pepper
- Salt

Directions:

1. Fit the oven with the rack in position 1. Grease 8-inch baking dish and set aside.
2. In a large bowl, whisk eggs with milk, pepper, and salt. Add remaining ingredients and stir well.
3. Pour egg mixture into the prepared baking dish.
4. Set to bake at 350 for 45 minutes, place the baking dish in the oven.
5. Serve and enjoy.

Sausage Veggie Egg Bake

 Time: 40 minutes   Serve: 4

Nutritional Value

(Amount per Serving):

Calories 655
Fat 50 g
Carbohydrates 12 g
Sugar 3 g
Protein 38 g
Cholesterol 502 mg

Ingredients:

- 10 eggs
- 1 cup pepper, diced
- 1 lb sausage, cut into 1/2-inch pieces
- 1 tsp garlic powder
- 1/2 cup almond milk
- 1 cup spinach, diced
- 1 cup onion, diced
- Pepper
- Salt

Directions:

1. Fit the oven with the rack in position 1. Grease 8-inch baking dish and set aside.
2. In a bowl, whisk eggs with milk and spices. Add vegetables and sausage and stir to combine.
3. Pour egg mixture into the prepared baking dish.
4. Set to bake at 400 for 30 minutes, place the baking dish in the oven.
5. Serve and enjoy.

Baked Donuts

⊕ **Time: 30 minutes**   🎩 **Serve: 6**

Nutritional Value

(Amount per Serving):

Calories 185
Fat 16 g
Carbohydrates 7 g
Sugar 1 g
Protein 5 g
Cholesterol 110 mg

Ingredients:

- 4 eggs
- 1/4 cup coconut oil
- 1/3 cup coconut flour
- 1/2 tsp baking soda
- 1/2 tsp baking powder
- 1/2 tsp instant coffee
- 1/3 cup almond milk
- 1 tbsp liquid stevia
- 3 tbsp cocoa powder

Directions:

1. Fit the oven with the rack in position 1. Grease donut pan and set aside.
2. Add all ingredients into the mixing bowl and mix until well combined.
3. Pour batter into the donut pan.
4. Set to bake at 350 for 20 minutes, place donut pan in the oven.
5. Serve and enjoy.

Healthy Broccoli Muffins

⊕ **Time: 40 minutes**   🔔 **Serve: 6**

Nutritional Value

(Amount per Serving):

Calories 356
Fat 30 g
Carbohydrates 13 g
Sugar 2 g
Protein 12 g
Cholesterol 54 mg

Ingredients:

- 2 eggs

- 1 cup broccoli florets, chopped

- 1 tsp baking powder

- 2 tbsp nutritional yeast

- 1 cup almond milk

- 2 cups almond flour

- 1/2 tsp sea salt

Directions:

1. Fit the oven with the rack in position 1. Grease 6-cups muffin tin and set aside.
2. Add all ingredients into the large bowl and whisk until well combined.
3. Pour egg mixture into the muffin tin.
4. Set to bake at 350 for 30 minutes, place muffin tin in the oven.
5. Serve and enjoy.

Easy Crust-less Quiche

 Time: 50 minutes   Serve: 6

Nutritional Value

(Amount per Serving):

Calories 166
Fat 11 g
Carbohydrates 3 g
Sugar 3 g
Protein 11 g
Cholesterol 185 mg

Ingredients:

- 6 eggs
- 1 cup milk
- 1 cup cheddar cheese, grated
- 1 cup tomatoes, chopped
- Pepper
- Salt

Directions:

1. Fit the oven with the rack in position 1. Grease 8-inch pie dish with and set aside.
2. In a bowl, whisk eggs with cheese, milk, pepper, and salt. Add tomatoes and stir well.
3. Pour egg mixture into the prepared pie dish.
4. Set to bake at 350 for 35 minutes, after 45 minutes, place the pie dish in the oven.
5. Serve and enjoy.

Cheese Frittata

 Time: 40 minutes 　  Serve: 6

Nutritional Value

(Amount per Serving):

Calories 75
Fat 5 g
Carbohydrates 1.1 g
Sugar 1 g
Protein 6 g
Cholesterol 165 mg

Ingredients:

- 6 eggs

- 1/2 cup tomatoes, chopped

- 2 tbsp water

- 3/4 cup mozzarella cheese

- 1/4 cup fresh basil, chopped

- Pepper

- Salt

Directions:

1. Fit the oven with the rack in position 1. Grease 8-inch pie dish and set aside.
2. In a bowl, whisk eggs with water, 1/2 cheese, pepper, and salt.
3. Add remaining cheese, basil, and tomatoes and stir well.
4. Pour egg mixture into the prepared pie dish.
5. Set to bake at 350 for 30 minutes, place pie dish in the oven.
6. Serve and enjoy.

Healthy Breakfast Egg Casserole

 Time: 30 minutes Serve: 4

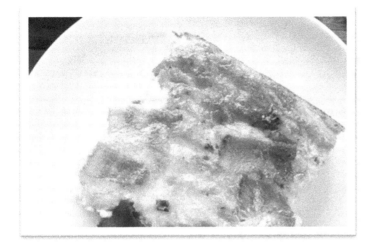

Nutritional Value

(Amount per Serving):

Calories 360
Fat 26 g
Carbohydrates 5 g
Sugar 2 g
Protein 20 g
Cholesterol 300 mg

Ingredients:

- 6 eggs
- 1/3 bell pepper, diced
- 2 bread slices, cubed
- 5 bacon slices, diced
- 1 cup cheddar cheese, shredded
- 1/2 tsp garlic, minced
- 3 tbsp milk
- 2 tbsp green onion, chopped
- Pepper
- Salt

Directions:

1. Fit the oven with the rack in position 1. Grease 8-inch baking dish and set aside.
2. Add all ingredients into the mixing bowl and stir until well combined. Pour into the prepared baking dish.
3. Set to bake at 350 for 20 minutes, place the baking dish in the oven.
4. Serve and enjoy.

Delicious Berry Oatmeal

⊕ **Time: 30 minutes**   🫐 **Serve: 4**

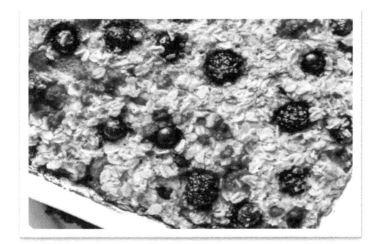

Nutritional Value

(Amount per Serving):

Calories 460
Fat 8 g
Carbohydrates 80.7 g
Sugar 22 g
Protein 15 g
Cholesterol 48 mg

Ingredients:

- 1 egg
- 1/2 cup blackberries
- 1/2 cup strawberries, sliced
- 2 cups old fashioned oats
- 1 cup blueberries
- 1/4 cup maple syrup
- 1 1/2 cups milk
- 1 1/2 tsp baking powder
- 1/2 tsp salt

Directions:

1. Fit the oven with the rack in position 1. Grease baking dish and set aside.
2. In a bowl, mix together oats, salt, and baking powder.
3. Add vanilla, egg, maple syrup, and milk and stir well.
4. Add berries and stir well.
5. Pour mixture into the baking dish.
6. Set to bake at 375 for 20 minutes, place the baking dish in the oven.
7. Serve and enjoy.

Italian Frittata

 Time: 40 minutes  Serve: 4

Nutritional Value

(Amount per Serving):

Calories 175
Fat 11 g
Carbohydrates 4 g
Sugar 2 g
Protein 15 g
Cholesterol 335 mg

Ingredients:

- 8 eggs

- 3 tbsp parmesan cheese, grated

- 2 zucchini, chopped and cooked

- 1 tbsp fresh parsley, chopped

- Pepper & salt, to taste

Directions:

1. Fit the oven with the rack in position 1. Grease baking dish and set aside.
2. In a mixing bowl, whisk eggs with pepper and salt.
3. Add parsley, cheese, and zucchini and stir well.
4. Pour egg mixture into the prepared baking dish.
5. Set to bake at 350 for 30 minutes, place the baking dish in the oven.
6. Serve and enjoy.

Herb Egg Muffins

 Time: 30 minutes    Serve: 6

Nutritional Value

(Amount per Serving):

Calories 68
Fat 5 g
Carbohydrates 0.8 g
Sugar 0.4 g
Protein 6 g
Cholesterol 164 mg

Ingredients:

- 6 eggs
- 1/4 cup mozzarella cheese, grated
- 1 tbsp fresh dill, chopped
- 1 tbsp fresh parsley, chopped
- 1 tbsp chives, chopped
- 1 tbsp fresh basil, chopped
- 1 tbsp fresh cilantro, chopped
- Pepper
- Salt

Directions:

1. Fit the oven with the rack in position 1. Grease 6-cups muffin tin and set aside.
2. In a bowl, whisk eggs with pepper and salt. Add remaining ingredients and stir well.
3. Pour egg mixture into the prepared muffin tin.
4. Set to bake at 350 for 20 minutes, place muffin tin in the oven.
5. Serve and enjoy.

POULTRY RECIPES

Greek Chicken

 Time: 40 minutes Serve: 4

Nutritional Value

(Amount per Serving):

Calories 312
Fat 20 g
Carbohydrates 2 g
Sugar 0.3 g
Protein 33 g
Cholesterol 100 mg

Ingredients:

- 1 lb chicken breasts, skinless & boneless
- For marinade:
- 3 garlic cloves, minced
- 1 tbsp lemon juice
- 3 tbsp olive oil
- 1/2 tsp dill
- 1 tsp onion powder
- 1/4 tsp basil
- 1/4 tsp oregano
- 1/4 tsp pepper
- 1/2 tsp salt

Directions:

1. Line the Baking Pan with foil and set aside.
2. Add all marinade ingredients into the bowl and mix well.
3. Add chicken into the marinade and coat well.
4. Cover and place in the refrigerator overnight.
5. Arrange marinated chicken onto the baking pan. Place the baking pan into rack position 2.
6. Set to Convection Bake at 400°F for 30 minutes.
7. Serve and enjoy.

Juicy Chicken Breast

⏀ **Time: 25 minutes**   🫕 **Serve: 8**

Nutritional Value

(Amount per Serving):

Calories 166
Fat 7 g
Carbohydrates 3 g
Sugar 2 g
Protein 22 g
Cholesterol 65 mg

Ingredients:

- 4 chicken breasts, skinless and boneless
- 1 tbsp olive oil
- For rub:
- 4 tsp brown sugar
- 4 tsp paprika
- 1 tsp garlic powder
- 1 tsp onion powder
- 1 tsp pepper
- 1 tsp salt

Directions:

1. Line the Baking Pan with foil and set aside.
2. Brush chicken breasts with olive oil.
3. In a small bowl, mix together rub ingredients and rub all over chicken breasts.
4. Arrange chicken breasts onto the baking pan roasting pan and bake. Place the baking pan into rack position 2.
5. Set to Convection Bake at 400°F for 15 minutes.
6. Serve and enjoy.

Baked Chicken Breasts

 Time: 35 minutes Serve: 6

Nutritional Value

(Amount per Serving):

Calories 320
Fat 16 g
Carbohydrates 0.4 g
Sugar 0.1 g
Protein 42 g
Cholesterol 130 mg

Ingredients:

- 6 chicken breasts, skinless & boneless
- 1 tsp Italian seasoning
- 2 tbsp olive oil
- 1/4 tsp pepper
- 1/4 tsp paprika
- 1/2 tsp garlic salt

Directions:

1. Line the Baking Pan with foil and set aside.
2. Brush chicken with oil.
3. Mix together Italian seasoning, garlic salt, paprika, and pepper and rub all over the chicken.
4. Arrange chicken breasts onto the baking pan. Place the baking pan into rack position 2.
5. Set to Convection Bake at 400°F for 25 minutes.
6. Slice and serve.

Flavors Chicken Thighs

 Time: 45 minutes   **Serve: 6**

Nutritional Value

(Amount per Serving):

Calories 320
Fat 15 g
Carbohydrates 0.3 g
Sugar 0 g
Protein 42 g
Cholesterol 130 mg

Ingredients:

- 6 chicken thighs
- 2 tbsp olive oil
- 2 tsp poultry seasoning
- Pepper
- Salt

Directions:

1. Line the Baking Pan with foil and set aside.
2. Brush chicken with oil and rub with poultry seasoning, pepper, and salt.
3. Arrange chicken onto the baking pan. Place the baking pan into rack position 2.
4. Set to Convection Bake at 400°F for 35 minutes.
5. Serve and enjoy.

Cheesy Parmesan Chicken

 Time: 45 minutes   Serve: 4

Nutritional Value

(Amount per Serving):

Calories 565
Fat 29 g
Carbohydrates 20 g
Sugar 1 g
Protein 53 g
Cholesterol 145 mg

Ingredients:

- 4 chicken breasts
- 1/4 cup olive oil
- 1 cup breadcrumbs
- 1 cup parmesan cheese, shredded
- Pepper
- Salt

Directions:

1. Line the Baking Pan with foil and set aside.
2. Season chicken with pepper and salt and brush with olive oil.
3. In a shallow dish, mix together parmesan cheese and breadcrumbs. Coat chicken with parmesan and breadcrumb mixture and place in the baking pan.
4. Place the baking pan into rack position 2.
5. Set to Convection Bake at 350°F for 35 minutes.
6. Serve and enjoy.

Curried Chicken

 Time: 50 minutes   Serve: 4

Nutritional Value

(Amount per Serving):

Calories 550
Fat 29 g
Carbohydrates 28 g
Sugar 24 g
Protein 45 g
Cholesterol 171 mg

Ingredients:

- 4 chicken breasts, skinless and boneless
- 1/3 cup butter
- 1/3 cup honey
- 4 tsp curry powder
- 1/4 cup mustard

Directions:

1. Line the Baking Pan with foil and set aside.
2. Add butter and honey in a small saucepan and heat over low heat until butter is melted.
3. Remove saucepan from heat and stir in curry powder and mustard.
4. Arrange chicken in a baking pan and pour butter mixture over chicken. Place the baking pan into rack position 2.
5. Set to Convection Bake at 375°F for 40 minutes.
6. Serve and enjoy.

BBQ Chicken Wings

⊕ **Time: 55 minutes**   🔔 **Serve: 6**

Nutritional Value

(Amount per Serving):

Calories 483

Fat 22 g

Carbohydrates 1.5 g

Sugar 0.2 g

Protein 66 g

Cholesterol 200 mg

Ingredients:

- 3 lbs chicken wings
- 1/2 cup dry BBQ spice rub
- 2 tbsp olive oil

1. Line the Baking Pan with foil and set aside.
2. Brush chicken wings with olive oil and place in a large bowl.
3. Add BBQ spice over chicken wings and toss well.
4. Arrange chicken wings on baking pan in a single layer. Place the baking pan into rack position 2.
5. Set to Convection Bake at 400°F for 45 minutes.
6. Serve and enjoy.

Directions:

Turkey Tenderloin

 Time: 55 minutes   Serve: 4

Nutritional Value

(Amount per Serving):

Calories 200
Fat 4 g
Carbohydrates 0.2 g
Sugar 0.1 g
Protein 42 g
Cholesterol 70 mg

Ingredients:

- 1 1/2 lbs turkey breast tenderloin
- 1 tsp Italian seasoning
- 1/2 tbsp olive oil
- 1/4 tsp pepper
- 1/2 tsp salt

Directions:

1. Line the Baking Pan with foil and set aside.
2. Brush turkey tenderloin with olive oil and rub with Italian seasoning, pepper, and salt.
3. Place tenderloin on a baking pan. Place the baking pan into rack position 2.
4. Set to Convection Bake at 390°F for 45 minutes.
5. Serve and enjoy.

Chicken Meatballs

 Time: 35 minutes    Serve: 4

Nutritional Value

(Amount per Serving):

Calories 386
Fat 19 g
Carbohydrates 11 g
Sugar 1 g
Protein 40 g
Cholesterol 150 mg

Ingredients:

- 1 lb ground chicken
- 1 egg, lightly beaten
- 2 tbsp olive oil
- 1 tbsp parsley, chopped
- 1/2 cup breadcrumbs
- 1/2 cup parmesan cheese, grated
- 1/4 tsp red pepper flakes
- 1/2 tsp dried oregano
- 1 tsp dried onion flakes
- 1 garlic clove, minced
- 1/4 tsp pepper
- 1/2 tsp sea salt

Directions:

1. Line the Baking Pan with foil and set aside.
2. Add all ingredients into the bowl and mix until just combined.
3. Make small balls from the meat mixture and place in the baking pan. Place the baking pan into rack position 2.
4. Set to Convection Bake at 400°F for 25 minutes.
5. Serve and enjoy.

Pesto Chicken

 Time: 35 minutes    Serve: 4

Nutritional Value

(Amount per Serving):

Calories 450
Fat 26 g
Carbohydrates 2 g
Sugar 2 g
Protein 49 g
Cholesterol 145 mg

Ingredients:

- 4 chicken breasts, skinless & boneless
- 1/2 cup pesto
- 1/2 cup parmesan cheese, shredded
- Pepper
- Salt

Directions:

1. Line the Baking Pan with foil and set aside.
2. Season chicken with pepper and salt and place onto the baking pan.
3. Spread pesto on top of the chicken and sprinkle with shredded cheese. Place the baking pan into rack position 2.
4. Set to Convection Bake at 400°F for 25 minutes.
5. Serve and enjoy.

Lemon Pepper Chicken

 Time: 40 minutes 　 Serve: 4

Nutritional Value

(Amount per Serving):

Calories 323
Fat 14 g
Carbohydrates 2 g
Sugar 1 g
Protein 43 g
Cholesterol 140 mg

Ingredients:

- 4 chicken breasts, skinless and boneless
- 1 tsp lemon pepper seasoning
- 4 tsp lemon juice
- 4 tsp butter, sliced
- 1/2 tsp paprika
- 1 tsp garlic powder
- Pepper
- Salt

Directions:

1. Line the Baking Pan with foil and set aside.
2. Season chicken with pepper and salt and place onto the baking pan.
3. Pour lemon juice over chicken.
4. Mix together paprika, garlic powder, and lemon pepper seasoning and sprinkle over chicken.
5. Add butter slices on top of the chicken. Place the baking pan into rack position 2.
6. Set to Convection Bake at 350°F for 30 minutes.
7. Serve and enjoy.

Meatballs

Time: 30 minutes   Serve: 6

Nutritional Value

(Amount per Serving):

Calories 215
Fat 10 g
Carbohydrates 8 g
Sugar 1 g
Protein 25 g
Cholesterol 132 mg

Ingredients:

- 1 lb ground turkey
- 1 tsp dried oregano
- 1 tbsp garlic, minced
- 1 tsp cumin
- 1 tbsp basil, chopped
- 1/3 cup coconut flour
- 2 cups zucchini, grated
- 1 tbsp dried onion flakes
- 2 eggs, lightly beaten
- 1 tbsp nutritional yeast
- Pepper
- Salt

Directions:

1. Line the Baking Pan with foil and set aside.
2. Add all ingredients into the bowl and mix until just combined.
3. Make small balls from the meat mixture and place onto the baking pan. Place the baking pan into rack position 2.
4. Set to Convection Bake at 400°F for 20 minutes.
5. Serve and enjoy.

Delicious Chicken Wings

🕐 **Time: 35 minutes**   🎩 **Serve: 4**

Nutritional Value

(Amount per Serving):

Calories 595
Fat 34 g
Carbohydrates 1 g
Sugar 1 g
Protein 66 g
Cholesterol 245 mg

Ingredients:

- 2 lbs chicken wings

- 6 tbsp butter, melted

- 12 oz hot sauce

- 1/2 tsp Worcestershire sauce

- 1/2 tsp Tabasco

Directions:

1. Place the air fryer Basket onto the Baking Pan and spray air fryer basket with cooking spray.
2. Add chicken wings into the air fryer basket.
3. Place assembled baking pan into Rack Position 2.
4. Set to air fry at 375°F for 25 minutes.
5. Meanwhile, in a bowl, mix together hot sauce, Worcestershire sauce, and butter. Set aside.
6. Add cooked chicken wings into the sauce bowl and toss well.
7. Serve and enjoy.

Chili Garlic Chicken Wings

 Time: 30 minutes　　　 Serve: 4

Nutritional Value

(Amount per Serving):

Calories 580
Fat 22 g
Carbohydrates 2 g
Sugar 0.3 g
Protein 87 g
Cholesterol 267 mg

Ingredients:

- 12 chicken wings

- 1 tsp granulated garlic

- 1 tbsp chili powder

- 1/2 tbsp baking powder

- 1/2 tsp sea salt

Directions:

1. Place the air fryer Basket onto the Baking Pan and spray air fryer basket with cooking spray.
2. Add chicken wings into the large bowl and toss with remaining ingredients.
3. Transfer chicken wings into the air fryer basket.
4. Place assembled baking pan into Rack Position 2.
5. Set to air fry at 400°F for 20 minutes.
6. Serve and enjoy.

Tasty Fajita Chicken

🕐 **Time: 25 minutes**   🔔 **Serve: 4**

Nutritional Value

(Amount per Serving):

Calories 374
Fat 18 g
Carbohydrates 8 g
Sugar 3 g
Protein 43 g
Cholesterol 130 mg

Ingredients:

- 4 chicken breasts, make horizontal cuts on each piece
- 1 onion, sliced
- 1 bell pepper, sliced
- 2 tbsp fajita seasoning
- 2 tbsp olive oil

Directions:

1. Place the air fryer Basket onto the Baking Pan and spray air fryer basket with cooking spray.
2. Rub oil and seasoning all over the chicken breast.
3. Place chicken into the air fryer basket and top with bell peppers and onion.
4. Place assembled baking pan into Rack Position 2.
5. Set to air fry at 375°F for 15 minutes.
6. Serve and enjoy.

Delicious Chicken Tenders

 Time: 22 minutes    Serve: 4

Nutritional Value

(Amount per Serving):

Calories 295
Fat 11 g
Carbohydrates 18 g
Sugar 1 g
Protein 30 g
Cholesterol 171 mg

Ingredients:

- 3 eggs, lightly beaten
- 1 lb chicken tenderloin
- 1/3 cup breadcrumb
- 2 tbsp olive oil
- 1/2 cup all-purpose flour
- Pepper
- Salt

Directions:

1. Place the air fryer Basket onto the Baking Pan and spray air fryer basket with cooking spray.
2. In a shallow dish, mix together flour, pepper, and salt. Add breadcrumbs in a separate shallow dish. Add egg in a small bowl.
3. Roll chicken in flour then dips in egg and coat with breadcrumbs.
4. Place coated chicken on the air fryer basket.
5. Place assembled baking pan into Rack Position 2.
6. Set to air fry at 350°F for 12 minutes.
7. Serve and enjoy.

Meatballs

⊕ **Time: 15 minutes**   🧢 **Serve: 6**

Nutritional Value

(Amount per Serving):

Calories 227

Fat 5 g

Carbohydrates 2 g

Sugar 0.3 g

Protein 42 g

Cholesterol 155 mg

Ingredients:

- 2 eggs

- 2 lbs ground chicken breast

- 1/2 cup ricotta cheese

- 1/4 cup fresh parsley, chopped

- 1/2 cup almond flour

- 1 tsp pepper

- 2 tsp salt

Directions:

1. Place the air fryer Basket onto the Baking Pan and spray air fryer basket with cooking spray.
2. Add all ingredients into the large bowl and mix until just combined.
3. Make small balls from meat mixture and place onto the air fryer basket.
4. Place assembled baking pan into Rack Position 2.
5. Set to air fry at 375°F for 10 minutes.
6. Serve and enjoy.

Turkey Meatballs

 Time: 22 minutes   Serve: 4

Nutritional Value

(Amount per Serving):

Calories 275
Fat 14 g
Carbohydrates 6 g
Sugar 0.7 g
Protein 34 g
Cholesterol 157 mg

Ingredients:

- 1 egg
- 1 lb ground turkey
- 1 garlic clove, minced
- 2 green onion, chopped
- 2 tbsp coconut flour
- 1/4 cup celery, chopped
- 1/4 cup carrots, grated
- Pepper
- Salt

Directions:

1. Place the air fryer Basket onto the Baking Pan and spray air fryer basket with cooking spray.
2. Add all ingredients into the large bowl and mix until just combined.
3. Make small balls from the meat mixture and place onto the air fryer basket.
4. Place assembled baking pan into Rack Position 2.
5. Set to air fry at 400°F for 12 minutes.
6. Serve and enjoy.

Herb Chicken Wings

🕐 **Time: 25 minutes**   🧢 **Serve: 4**

Nutritional Value

(Amount per Serving):

Calories 475
Fat 19 g
Carbohydrates 1 g
Sugar 0.1 g
Protein 70 g
Cholesterol 211 mg

Ingredients:

- 2 lbs chicken wings

- 1 tsp herb de Provence

- 1 tsp paprika

- 1/2 cup parmesan cheese, grated

- Salt

Directions:

1. Place the air fryer Basket onto the Baking Pan and spray air fryer basket with cooking spray.
2. In a small bowl, mix together cheese, herb de Provence, paprika, and salt.
3. Coat chicken wings with cheese mixture and place onto the air fryer basket.
4. Place assembled baking pan into Rack Position 2.
5. Set to air fry at 350°F for 15 minutes.
6. Serve and enjoy.

Parmesan Chicken Nuggets

🕐 **Time: 18 minutes**   🎩 **Serve: 4**

Nutritional Value

(Amount per Serving):

Calories 160
Fat 6 g
Carbohydrates 10 g
Sugar 1 g
Protein 14 g
Cholesterol 39 mg

Ingredients:

- 2 chicken breast, boneless and cut into 1-inch pieces
- 1/2 cup breadcrumbs
- 1 tsp Italian seasoning
- 2 tbsp parmesan cheese, grated
- 1 tbsp olive oil
- Pepper
- Salt

Directions:

1. Line the Baking Pan with foil and set aside.
2. In a bowl, mix together breadcrumbs, Italian seasoning, cheese, pepper, and salt.
3. Brush chicken pieces with oil and coat with breadcrumbs.
4. Arrange coated chicken pieces onto the air fryer basket.
5. Place the baking pan into rack position 2.
6. Set to Convection Bake at 400°F for 8 minutes.
7. Serve and enjoy.

Sweet & Spicy Chicken Wings

 Time: 35 minutes   Serve: 2

Nutritional Value

(Amount per Serving):

Calories 400

Fat 15 g

Carbohydrates 5 g

Sugar 4 g

Protein 58 g

Cholesterol 178 mg

Ingredients:

- 10 chicken wings
- 2 tbsp chili sauce
- 1/2 tbsp honey
- 1/2 tbsp fresh lime juice
- Pepper
- Salt

Directions:

1. Place the air fryer Basket onto the Baking Pan and spray air fryer basket with cooking spray.
2. In a bowl, add chicken wings, chili sauce, lime juice, honey, pepper, and salt and toss well.
3. Arrange chicken wings onto the air fryer basket.
4. Place assembled baking pan into Rack Position 2.
5. Set to air fry at 350°F for 25 minutes.
6. Serve and enjoy.

Tasty Chicken Fritters

 Time: 20 minutes   Serve: 4

Nutritional Value

(Amount per Serving):

Calories 312
Fat 11 g
Carbohydrates 12 g
Sugar 1 g
Protein 38 g
Cholesterol 110 mg

Ingredients:

- 1 lb ground chicken
- 1/2 cup parmesan cheese, shredded
- 1 tsp onion powder
- 1 tsp garlic powder
- 1 tbsp dill, chopped
- 1/2 cup breadcrumbs
- 2 tbsp green onions, chopped
- Pepper
- Salt

Directions:

1. Place the air fryer Basket onto the Baking Pan and spray air fryer basket with cooking spray.
2. Add all ingredients into the bowl and mix until just combined.
3. Make patties from chicken mixture and place onto the air fryer basket.
4. Place assembled baking pan into Rack Position 2.
5. Set to air fry at 350°F for 10 minutes.
6. Serve and enjoy.

Rosemary Chicken

 Time: 35 minutes    Serve: 4

Nutritional Value

(Amount per Serving):

Calories 285
Fat 15 g
Carbohydrates 2 g
Sugar 0.3 g
Protein 33 g
Cholesterol 101 mg

Ingredients:

- 1 lb chicken breasts, skinless, boneless, and cubed
- 1 tbsp rosemary, chopped
- 1 tbsp garlic, minced
- 2 tbsp olive oil
- 2 tbsp chives, chopped
- 1 tbsp fresh lemon juice
- 1 tsp garlic powder
- Pepper
- Salt

Directions:

1. Place the air fryer Basket onto the Baking Pan and spray air fryer basket with cooking spray.
2. Add all ingredients into the bowl and toss well.
3. Transfer chicken mixture onto the air fryer basket.
4. Place assembled baking pan into Rack Position 2.
5. Set to air fry at 370°F for 25 minutes.
6. Serve and enjoy.

Delicious Turkey Burgers

 Time: 35 minutes   Serve: 9

Nutritional Value

(Amount per Serving):

Calories 122
Fat 6 g
Carbohydrates 3 g
Sugar 0.4 g
Protein 15 g
Cholesterol 70 mg

Ingredients:

- 1 egg, lightly beaten
- 2 tbsp lemon juice
- 2 tbsp cilantro, chopped
- 1 lb ground turkey
- 1/2 tsp garlic, minced
- 1/3 cup breadcrumbs
- 1 tsp creole seasoning
- Pepper
- Salt

Directions:

1. Place the air fryer Basket onto the Baking Pan and spray air fryer basket with cooking spray.
2. Add all ingredients into the bowl and mix until well combined.
3. Make small patties from meat mixture and place onto the air fryer basket.
4. Place assembled baking pan into Rack Position 2.
5. Set to air fry at 400°F for 25 minutes.
6. Serve and enjoy.

Easy Cajun Chicken

 Time: 20 minutes  Serve: 2

Nutritional Value

(Amount per Serving):

Calories 327
Fat 12 g
Carbohydrates 0 g
Sugar 0 g
Protein 50 g
Cholesterol 153 mg

Ingredients:

- 2 chicken breasts, skinless & boneless
- 3 tbsp Cajun spice

Directions:

1. Place the air fryer Basket onto the Baking Pan and spray air fryer basket with cooking spray.
2. Season chicken with Cajun spice and place onto the air fryer basket.
3. Place assembled baking pan into Rack Position 2.
4. Set to air fry at 350°F for 10 minutes.
5. Serve and enjoy.

SEAFOOD RECIPES

Delicious Cajun Salmon

 Time: 22 minutes 　　 Serve: 4

Nutritional Value

(Amount per Serving):

Calories 271
Fat 10 g
Carbohydrates 8 g
Sugar 8 g
Protein 34 g
Cholesterol 78 mg

Ingredients:

- 4 salmon fillets
- 4 tbsp brown sugar
- 2 tsp Cajun seasoning
- Salt

Directions:

1. Line the Baking Pan with foil and set aside.
2. Mix together Cajun seasoning, brown sugar, and salt and rub all over salmon.
3. Place salmon on the baking pan.
4. Place the baking pan into rack position 2.
5. Set to Convection Bake at 400°F for 12 minutes.
6. Serve and enjoy.

Flavors Lemon Cod

⊕ **Time: 30 minutes**   🔔 **Serve: 4**

Nutritional Value

(Amount per Serving):

Calories 309
Fat 20 g
Carbohydrates 2 g
Sugar 0.6 g
Protein 31 g
Cholesterol 114 mg

Ingredients:

- 1 1/2 lb cod fillet
- 2 lemon juice
- 2 tbsp olive oil
- 1 lemon, sliced
- 1/4 cup butter, diced
- 4 garlic cloves, minced
- Pepper
- Salt

Directions:

1. Line the Baking Pan with foil and set aside.
2. Place fish fillets in the baking pan and season with pepper and salt.
3. Whisk together garlic, lemon juice, and oil and pour over fish fillets.
4. Arrange butter pieces and lemon slices on top of fish fillets.
5. Place the baking pan into rack position 2.
6. Set to Convection Bake at 400°F for 20 minutes.
7. Serve and enjoy.

Spicy Tilapia

 Time: 25 minutes   Serve: 4

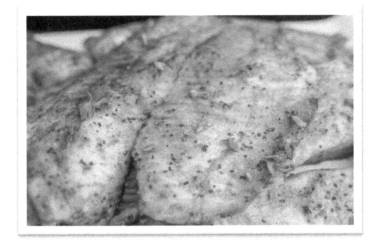

Nutritional Value

(Amount per Serving):

Calories 149
Fat 12 g
Carbohydrates 4 g
Sugar 0.1 g
Protein 6 g
Cholesterol 38 mg

Ingredients:

- 4 tilapia fillets
- 1/2 tsp red chili powder
- 1 tsp garlic, minced
- 3 tbsp butter, melted
- 1 tbsp fresh lemon juice
- 2 tsp fresh parsley, chopped
- 1 lemon, sliced
- Pepper
- Salt

Directions:

1. Line the Baking Pan with foil and set aside.
2. Place fish fillets in the baking pan and season with pepper and salt.
3. Mix together butter, red chili powder, garlic, and lemon juice and pour over fish fillets.
4. Arrange lemon slices on top of fish fillets.
5. Place the baking pan into rack position 2.
6. Set to Convection Bake at 350°F for 15 minutes.
7. Garnish with parsley and serve.

Crab Cakes

 Time: 40 minutes    Serve: 6

Nutritional Value

(Amount per Serving):

Calories 156
Fat 12 g
Carbohydrates 12 g
Sugar 2 g
Protein 12 g
Cholesterol 43 mg

Ingredients:

- 16 oz lump crab meat
- 1 tsp old bay seasoning
- 1 tsp brown mustard
- 2/3 cup mashed avocado
- 1/4 cup celery, diced
- 1/4 cup onion, diced
- 1 cup crushed crackers

Directions:

1. Line the Baking Pan with foil and set aside.
2. Add all ingredients into the bowl and mix until just combined.
3. Make small patties from mixture and place on a baking pan.
4. Place the baking pan into rack position 2.
5. Set to Convection Bake at 350°F for 30 minutes.
6. Serve and enjoy.

Garlic Lime Shrimp

 Time: 20 minutes    Serve: 4

Nutritional Value

(Amount per Serving):

Calories 195
Fat 7.7 g
Carbohydrates 4.4 g
Sugar 0.4 g
Protein 26.1 g
Cholesterol 254 mg

Ingredients:

- 1 lb shrimp, peel and deveined
- 2 tbsp lime juice
- 2 tbsp butter, melted
- 1/4 cup fresh cilantro, chopped
- 3 garlic cloves, pressed

Directions:

1. Line the Baking Pan with foil and set aside.
2. Add shrimp into the baking dish.
3. Mix together garlic, lime juice, and butter and pour over shrimp.
4. Toss shrimp well and let it sit for 15 minutes.
5. Place the baking pan into rack position 2.
6. Set to Convection Bake at 375°F for 15 minutes.
7. Garnish with cilantro and serve.

Dijon Salmon

 Time: 22 minutes   Serve: 4

Nutritional Value

(Amount per Serving):

Calories 360
Fat 18 g
Carbohydrates 14 g
Sugar 12 g
Protein 35 g
Cholesterol 78 mg

Ingredients:

- 4 salmon fillets
- 1/4 cup Dijon mustard
- 1/4 cup maple syrup
- 2 garlic cloves, minced
- 2 tbsp olive oil
- Pepper
- Salt

Directions:

1. Line the Baking Pan with foil and set aside.
2. Place salmon fillets into the baking pan.
3. Mix together garlic, olive oil, Dijon mustard, maple syrup, pepper, and salt and pour over salmon. Coat well and let sit for 10 minutes.
4. Place the baking pan into rack position 2.
5. Set to Convection Bake at 400°F for 12 minutes.
6. Serve and enjoy.

Tasty Shrimp Fajitas

🕐 Time: 25 minutes   🎩 Serve: 4

Nutritional Value

(Amount per Serving):

Calories 229
Fat 8 g
Carbohydrates 12 g
Sugar 5 g
Protein 27 g
Cholesterol 240 mg

Ingredients:

- 1 lb shrimp, peeled and deveined
- 3 bell peppers, sliced
- 1 medium onion, sliced
- 1/2 lime juice
- 1 1/2 tbsp taco seasoning
- 1 1/2 tbsp olive oil

Directions:

1. Line the Baking Pan with foil and set aside.
2. In a bowl, toss shrimp with remaining ingredients.
3. Spread shrimp mixture on a baking pan.
4. Place the baking pan into rack position 2.
5. Set to Convection Bake at 400°F for 15 minutes.
6. Serve and enjoy.

Parmesan Walnut Salmon

 Time: 25 minutes    Serve: 4

Nutritional Value

(Amount per Serving):

Calories 312
Fat 18 g
Carbohydrates 1 g
Sugar 0.2 g
Protein 38 g
Cholesterol 83 mg

Ingredients:

- 4 salmon fillets

- 1/4 cup walnuts

- 1 tsp olive oil

- 1/4 cup parmesan cheese, grated

- 1 tbsp lemon rind

Directions:

1. Line the Baking Pan with foil and set aside.
2. Place salmon fillets in the baking pan.
3. Add walnuts into the blender and blend until ground.
4. Mix together walnuts, cheese, oil, and lemon rind and spread on top of salmon fillets.
5. Place the baking pan into rack position 2.
6. Set to Convection Bake at 400°F for 15 minutes.
7. Serve and enjoy.

Greek Pesto Salmon

 Time: 30 minutes  Serve: 4

Nutritional Value

(Amount per Serving):

Calories 447
Fat 28 g
Carbohydrates 8 g
Sugar 6 g
Protein 41 g
Cholesterol 103 mg

Ingredients:

- 4 salmon fillets
- 1/2 cup pesto
- 1/2 cup feta cheese, crumbled
- 2 cups grape tomatoes, halved
- 1 onion, chopped

Directions:

1. Line the Baking Pan with foil and set aside.
2. Place salmon fillet in baking pan and top with tomatoes, onion, pesto, and cheese.
3. Place the baking pan into rack position 2.
4. Set to Convection Bake at 350°F for 20 minutes.
5. Serve and enjoy.

Easy Baked Tilapia

 Time: 20 minutes　　 Serve: 4

Nutritional Value

(Amount per Serving):

Calories 160
Fat 8 g
Carbohydrates 1 g
Sugar 0.1 g
Protein 21 g

Cholesterol 55 mg

Ingredients:

- 1 lb tilapia fillets

- 2 tbsp garlic, minced

- 2 tbsp olive oil

- 2 tbsp dried parsley

- Pepper

- Salt

1. Line the Baking Pan with foil and set aside.
2. Place fish fillets on a baking pan. Drizzle with oil and season with pepper and salt.
3. Sprinkle garlic and parsley over fish fillets.
4. Place the baking pan into rack position 2.
5. Set to Convection Bake at 400°F for 15 minutes.
6. Serve and enjoy.

Directions:

Cajun Catfish Fillets

 Time: 20 minutes   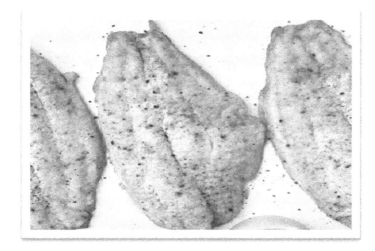 Serve: 4

Nutritional Value

(Amount per Serving):

Calories 165
Fat 9 g
Carbohydrates 2 g
Sugar 0.6 g
Protein 18 g
Cholesterol 53 mg

Ingredients:

- 1 lb catfish fillets, cut ½-inch thick
- 1/2 tsp ground cumin
- 3/4 tsp chili powder
- 1 tsp crushed red pepper
- 2 tsp onion powder
- 1 tbsp dried oregano, crushed
- Pepper
- Salt

Directions:

1. Line the Baking Pan with foil and set aside.
2. In a small bowl, mix together cumin, chili powder, crushed red pepper, onion powder, oregano, pepper, and salt.
3. Rub fish fillets with the spice mixture on both sides.
4. Place fish fillets in a baking pan.
5. Place the baking pan into rack position 2.
6. Set to Convection Bake at 350°F for 15 minutes.
7. Serve and enjoy.

Blackened Mahi Mahi

🕐 Time: 17 minutes   🧢 Serve: 4

Nutritional Value

(Amount per Serving):

Calories 189
Fat 12 g
Carbohydrates 2 g
Sugar 0.5 g
Protein 19 g
Cholesterol 86 mg

Ingredients:

- 4 Mahi Mahi fillets

- 1 tsp paprika

- 1 tsp garlic powder

- 3 tbsp Olive oil

- 1/2 cayenne

- 1 tsp oregano

- 1 tsp cumin

- 1 tsp onion powder

- 1/2 tsp pepper

- 1/2 tsp salt

Directions:

1. Line the Baking Pan with foil and set aside.
2. Place fish fillets on the baking pan and drizzle with oil.
3. In a small bowl, mix together cumin, onion powder, paprika, cayenne, oregano, garlic powder, pepper, and salt.
4. Rub fish fillets with a spice mixture.
5. Place the baking pan into rack position 2.

6. Set to Convection Bake at 450°F for 12 minutes.

7. Serve and enjoy.

Salmon Patties

 Time: 17 minutes   ... Serve: 2

Nutritional Value

(Amount per Serving):

Calories 184
Fat 9 g
Carbohydrates 1 g
Sugar 0.5 g
Protein 25 g
Cholesterol 132 mg

Ingredients:

- 1 egg, lightly beaten
- 8 oz salmon fillet, minced
- 1/4 tsp garlic powder
- 1/4 tsp onion powder
- Pepper
- Salt

Directions:

1. Place the air fryer Basket onto the Baking Pan and spray air fryer basket with cooking spray.
2. Add all ingredients into the bowl and mix until just combined.
3. Make small patties from salmon mixture and place onto the air fryer basket.
4. Place assembled baking pan into Rack Position 2.
5. Set to air fry at 400°F for 7 minutes.
6. Serve and enjoy.

Crab Cakes

 Time: 17 minutes 　  Serve: 2

Nutritional Value
(Amount per Serving):

Calories 151
Fat 4 g
Carbohydrates 21 g
Sugar 5 g
Protein 6 g
Cholesterol 9 mg

Ingredients:

- 1 large egg whites

- 2 green onions, chopped

- 1/2 celery rib, chopped

- 3/4 cup crabmeat, drained

- 1/4 cup breadcrumbs

- 1 1/2 tbsp mayonnaise

- 1/2 sweet red pepper, chopped

- 1/8 tsp salt

1. Place the air fryer Basket onto the Baking Pan and spray air fryer basket with cooking spray.
2. Place bread crumbs in a shallow dish.
3. In a bowl, add remaining ingredients except for crabmeat and mix well. Gently fold in crabmeat.
4. Drop a tablespoon of crabmeat mixture to the breadcrumbs and slowly coat and shape into patties.
5. Place crab cakes onto the air fryer basket.
6. Place assembled baking pan into Rack Position 2.
7. Set to air fry at 375°F for 12 minutes.
8. Serve and enjoy.

Directions:

Salmon Dill Patties

⊕ **Time: 15 minutes**　　⬤ **Serve: 2**

Nutritional Value

(Amount per Serving):

Calories 350
Fat 18 g
Carbohydrates 3 g
Sugar 1 g
Protein 44 g
Cholesterol 172 mg

Ingredients:

- 1 egg

- 1 tsp dill weed

- 1/2 cup almond flour

- 14 oz salmon

- 1/4 cup onion, diced

1. Place the air fryer Basket onto the Baking Pan and spray air fryer basket with cooking spray.
2. Add all ingredients into the bowl and mix well.
3. Make patties from bowl mixture and place onto the air fryer basket.
4. Place assembled baking pan into Rack Position 2.
5. Set to air fry at 375°F for 10 minutes.
6. Serve and enjoy.

Directions:

Spicy Shrimp

 Time: 16 minutes 　　  Serve: 2

Nutritional Value

(Amount per Serving):

Calories 197
Fat 9 g
Carbohydrates 2 g
Sugar 0.1 g
Protein 26 g
Cholesterol 239 mg

Ingredients:

- 1/2 lb shrimp, peeled and deveined
- 1/2 tsp old bay seasoning
- 1/2 tsp cayenne pepper
- 1 tbsp olive oil
- 1/4 tsp paprika
- Pinch of salt

Directions:

1. Place the air fryer Basket onto the Baking Pan and spray air fryer basket with cooking spray.
2. Add shrimp and remaining ingredients into the bowl and toss well to coat.
3. Add shrimp into the air fryer basket.
4. Place assembled baking pan into Rack Position 2.
5. Set to air fry at 400°F for 6 minutes.
6. Serve and enjoy.

Air Fried White Fish Fillet

🕐 **Time: 20 minutes**   🧢 **Serve: 2**

Nutritional Value

(Amount per Serving):

Calories 298
Fat 13 g
Carbohydrates 1.4 g
Sugar 0.4 g
Protein 42 g
Cholesterol 131 mg

Ingredients:

- 12 oz white fish fillets
- 1/2 tsp lemon pepper seasoning
- 1/2 tsp garlic powder
- 1/2 tsp onion powder
- Pepper
- Salt

Directions:

1. Place the air fryer Basket onto the Baking Pan and spray air fryer basket with cooking spray.
2. Spray fish fillets with cooking spray and season with onion powder, lemon pepper seasoning, garlic powder, pepper, and salt.
3. Place parchment paper in the bottom of the air fryer basket.
4. Place fish fillets into the air fryer basket.
5. Place assembled baking pan into Rack Position 2.
6. Set to air fry at 350°F for 10 minutes.
7. Serve and enjoy.

Coconut Shrimp

⊕ **Time: 18 minutes**   🧢 **Serve: 8**

Nutritional Value

(Amount per Serving):

Calories 112
Fat 5 g
Carbohydrates 5 g
Sugar 0.7 g
Protein 13 g
Cholesterol 122 mg

Ingredients:

- 2 eggs, lightly beaten
- 1 lb large shrimp, peeled and deveined
- 1 cup flaked coconut
- 1/4 cup coconut flour

Directions:

1. Place the air fryer Basket onto the Baking Pan and spray air fryer basket with cooking spray.
2. In a small bowl, add coconut flour.
3. In a shallow bowl, add eggs. In a separate shallow bowl, add flaked coconut.
4. Coat shrimp with coconut flour then dip in eggs and finally coat with flaked coconut.
5. Place coated shrimp into the air fryer basket.

6. Place assembled baking pan into Rack Position 2.

7. Set to air fry at 400°F for 8 minutes.

8. Serve and enjoy.

Parmesan Fish Fillets

 Time: 20 minutes  Serve: 4

Nutritional Value

(Amount per Serving):

Calories 220
Fat 10 g
Carbohydrates 1 g
Sugar 0.1 g
Protein 30 g
Cholesterol 92 mg

Ingredients:

- 1 lb white fish fillets

- 1/2 tsp lemon pepper seasoning

- 1/4 cup coconut flour

- 1/4 cup parmesan cheese

Directions:

1. Place the air fryer Basket onto the Baking Pan and spray air fryer basket with cooking spray.
2. In a shallow dish, mix together coconut flour, parmesan cheese, and lemon pepper seasoning.
3. Spray white fish fillets from both sides with cooking spray.
4. Coat fish fillets with coconut flour mixture.
5. Place coated fish fillets into the air fryer basket.
6. Place assembled baking pan into Rack Position 2.
7. Set to air fry at 400°F for 10 minutes.
8. Serve and enjoy.

Shrimp Fajitas

 Time: 33 minutes 🧢 Serve: 12

Nutritional Value

(Amount per Serving):

Calories 55
Fat 1 g
Carbohydrates 3 g
Sugar 1 g
Protein 9 g
Cholesterol 80 mg

Ingredients:

- 1 lb shrimp, tail-off
- 1 green bell pepper, diced
- 1 red bell pepper, diced
- 2 tbsp taco seasoning
- 1/2 cup onion, diced

Directions:

1. Place the air fryer Basket onto the Baking Pan and spray air fryer basket with cooking spray.
2. Add shrimp, taco seasoning, onion, and bell peppers into the bowl and toss well.
3. Place shrimp mixture into the air fryer basket.
4. Place assembled baking pan into Rack Position 2.
5. Set to air fry at 350°F for 12 minutes.
6. Serve and enjoy.

Chipotle Shrimp

⊕ **Time: 18 minutes**   🧢 **Serve: 4**

Nutritional Value
(Amount per Serving):

Calories 274
Fat 10 g
Carbohydrates 6 g
Sugar 1 g
Protein 39 g
Cholesterol 359 mg

Ingredients:

- 1 1/2 lbs shrimp, peeled and deveined

- 2 tsp chipotle in adobo

- 2 tbsp olive oil

- 4 tbsp lime juice

- 1 /4 tsp ground cumin

Directions:

1. Place the air fryer Basket onto the Baking Pan and spray air fryer basket with cooking spray.
2. Add shrimp, oil, lime juice, cumin, and chipotle in a zip-lock bag.
3. Seal bag shake well and place it in the refrigerator for 30 minutes.
4. Thread marinated shrimp onto skewers and place skewers into the air fryer basket.
5. Place assembled baking pan into Rack Position 2.
6. Set to air fry at 350°F for 8 minutes.
7. Serve and enjoy.

Air Fried Crab Cakes

🕐 **Time: 20 minutes**　　🔔 **Serve: 4**

Nutritional Value

(Amount per Serving):

Calories 136
Fat 13.7 g
Carbohydrates 2.8 g
Sugar 0.5 g
Protein 10.3 g
Cholesterol 89 mg

Ingredients:

- 8 oz lump crab meat
- 1 egg, lightly beaten
- 1/2 tsp old bay seasoning
- 1 green onion, sliced
- 2 tbsp parsley, chopped
- 1/4 cup almond flour
- 2 tbsp butter, melted
- 2 tsp Dijon mustard
- 1 tbsp mayonnaise
- Pepper
- Salt

Directions:

1. Place the air fryer Basket onto the Baking Pan and spray air fryer basket with cooking spray.
2. Add crab meat, mustard, mayonnaise, egg, old bay seasoning, green onion, parsley, almond flour, pepper, and salt into the bowl and mix until just combined.
3. Make four equal shapes of patties from mixture and place on a waxed paper-lined dish and refrigerate for 30 minutes.
4. Brush melted butter over both sides of patties and place into the air fryer basket.
5. Place assembled baking pan into Rack Position 2.
6. Set to air fry at 350°F for 10 minutes.
7. Serve and enjoy.

Garlic Butter Shrimp

 Time: 16 minutes    Serve: 4

Nutritional Value

(Amount per Serving):

Calories 99
Fat 9 g
Carbohydrates 1 g
Sugar 0 g
Protein 4 g
Cholesterol 58 mg

Ingredients:

- 12 large shrimp, peeled and deveined
- 3 tbsp butter, melted
- 3 garlic cloves, minced
- Pepper
- Salt

Directions:

1. Place the air fryer Basket onto the Baking Pan and spray air fryer basket with cooking spray.
2. In a bowl, add shrimp, garlic, butter, pepper, and salt and marinate shrimp for 15 minutes.
3. Remove shrimp from marinade and place into the air fryer basket.
4. Place assembled baking pan into Rack Position 2.
5. Set to air fry at 350°F for 6 minutes.
6. Serve and enjoy.

Tasty Shrimp Fajitas

🕐 **Time: 18 minutes**   🎩 **Serve: 4**

Nutritional Value

(Amount per Serving):

Calories 173
Fat 4 g
Carbohydrates 13 g
Sugar 6 g
Protein 21 g
Cholesterol 233 mg

Ingredients:

- 1 lb jumbo shrimp, peeled and deveined
- 1 oz fajita seasoning
- 2 garlic cloves, minced
- 1 tbsp olive oil
- 1 onion, sliced
- 1 yellow bell pepper, sliced
- 1 red bell pepper, sliced
- 1 tsp chili powder
- 1 tsp paprika

Directions:

1. Place the air fryer Basket onto the Baking Pan and spray air fryer basket with cooking spray.
2. Add shrimp and remaining ingredients into the large bowl and toss well.
3. Add shrimp mixture into the air fryer basket.
4. Place assembled baking pan into Rack Position 2.
5. Set to air fry at 400°F for 8 minutes.
6. Serve and enjoy.

Herb Salmon

🕐 **Time: 15 minutes**   🧢 **Serve: 2**

Nutritional Value

(Amount per Serving):

Calories 305
Fat 24 g
Carbohydrates 1 g
Sugar 0 g
Protein 22 g
Cholesterol 58 mg

Ingredients:

- 8 oz salmon fillets

- 1 tbsp lemon herb butter

- 1/4 tsp paprika

- 1 tsp Herb de Provence

- 2 tbsp olive oil

- Pepper

- Salt

Directions:

1. Place the air fryer Basket onto the Baking Pan and spray air fryer basket with cooking spray.
2. In a small bowl, mix together paprika, Herb de Provence, pepper, and salt.
3. Rub salmon fillets with oil and spice mixture.
4. Place salmon fillets into the air fryer basket.
5. Place assembled baking pan into Rack Position 2.
6. Set to air fry at 400°F for 5 minutes.
7. Melt lemon herb butter and pour over salmon.
8. Serve immediately and enjoy.

SNACKS & APPETIZERS

Potato Wedges

 Time: 25 minutes   Serve: 4

Nutritional Value

(Amount per Serving):

Calories 120
Fat 5 g
Carbohydrates 17 g
Sugar 1 g
Protein 2 g
Cholesterol 0 mg

Ingredients:

- 2 medium potatoes, cut into wedges
- 1/2 tsp paprika
- 1 1/2 tbsp olive oil
- 1/8 tsp cayenne pepper
- 1/4 tsp garlic powder
- 1/4 tsp pepper
- 1 tsp sea salt

Directions:

1. Place the air fryer Basket onto the Baking Pan and spray air fryer basket with cooking spray.
2. Soak potato wedges into the water for 30 minutes. Drain well and pat dry with a paper towel.
3. In a bowl, toss potato wedges with remaining ingredients.

4. Place assembled baking pan into Rack Position 2.

5. Set to air fry at 400°F for 15 minutes.
6. Serve and enjoy.

Tasty Ranch Potatoes

 Time: 30 minutes    Serve: 2

Nutritional Value

(Amount per Serving):

Calories 99
Fat 4 g
Carbohydrates 15 g
Sugar 0.2 g
Protein 3 g
Cholesterol 0 mg

Ingredients:

- 1/2 lb baby potatoes, wash and cut in half
- 1/4 tsp paprika
- 1/4 tsp onion powder
- 1/4 tsp garlic powder
- 1/4 tsp parsley
- 1/2 tbsp olive oil
- 1/4 tsp dill
- 1/4 tsp chives
- Salt

Directions:

1. Place the air fryer Basket onto the baking Pan and spray air fryer basket with cooking spray.
2. Add all ingredients into the bowl and toss well.
3. Spread potatoes on an air fryer basket.
4. Place assembled baking pan into Rack Position 2.
5. Set to air fry at 400°F for 20 minutes.
6. Serve and enjoy.

Spicy Cheese Dip

⏲ **Time: 40 minutes**   🎩 **Serve: 10**

Nutritional Value

(Amount per Serving):

Calories 348
Fat 32 g
Carbohydrates 3 g
Sugar 0.7 g
Protein 12 g
Cholesterol 96 mg

Ingredients:

- 16 oz cream cheese, softened
- 1 cup sour cream
- 1/2 cup hot salsa
- 3 cups cheddar cheese, shredded

1. Fit the oven with the rack in position 1. Grease 8-inch baking dish and set aside.
2. In a bowl, mix together all ingredients until just combined and pour into the baking dish.
3. Set to bake at 350 for 30 minutes, place the baking dish in the oven.
4. Serve and enjoy.

Directions:

Zucchini Patties

 Time: 35 minutes  Serve: 6

Nutritional Value

(Amount per Serving):

Calories 68
Fat 2 g
Carbohydrates 8 g
Sugar 1 g
Protein 3 g
Cholesterol 30 mg

Ingredients:

- 1 egg, lightly beaten
- 1 cup zucchini, shredded and squeeze out all liquid
- 1/4 tsp red pepper flakes
- 1/4 cup parmesan cheese, grated
- 2 tbsp onion, minced
- 1/2 tbsp Dijon mustard
- 1/2 tbsp mayonnaise
- 1/2 cup breadcrumbs
- Pepper
- Salt

Directions:

1. Place the air fryer Basket onto the Baking Pan and spray air fryer basket with cooking spray.
2. Add all ingredients into the bowl and mix until well combined.
3. Make small patties from the zucchini mixture and place it on an air fryer basket.
4. Place assembled baking pan into Rack Position 2.
5. Set to air fry at 400°F for 25 minutes.
6. Serve and enjoy.

Sweet Potato Fries

 Time: 26 minutes    Serve: 2

Nutritional Value

(Amount per Serving):

Calories 238
Fat 7 g
Carbohydrates 42 g
Sugar 1 g
Protein 2 g
Cholesterol 0 mg

Ingredients:

- 2 sweet potatoes, peeled and cut into fries shape
- 1 tbsp olive oil
- 1/4 tsp chili powder
- Salt

Directions:

1. Place the air fryer Basket onto the Baking Pan and spray air fryer basket with cooking spray.
2. In a bowl, add sweet potato fries, chili powder, garlic powder, olive oil, and salt and toss until well coated.
3. Arrange sweet potato fries on an air fryer basket.
4. Place assembled baking pan into Rack Position 2.
5. Set to air fry at 375°F for 16 minutes.
6. Serve and enjoy.

Cinnamon Maple Chickpeas

 Time: 22 minutes    Serve: 4

Nutritional Value

(Amount per Serving):

Calories 170
Fat 4 g
Carbohydrates 27 g
Sugar 3 g
Protein 5 g
Cholesterol 0 mg

Ingredients:

- 15 oz can chickpeas, rinsed, drained and pat dry
- 1 tbsp olive oil
- 1/2 tsp ground cinnamon
- 1 tbsp maple syrup
- Pepper
- Salt

1. Place the air fryer Basket onto the Baking Pan and spray air fryer basket with cooking spray.
2. Spread chickpeas on air fryer basket.
3. Place assembled baking pan into Rack Position 2.
4. Set to air fry at 375°F for 12 minutes.
5. In a large bowl, mix together cinnamon, maple syrup, oil, pepper, and salt. Add chickpeas and toss well.
6. Serve and enjoy.

Directions:

Spicy Chickpeas

🕐 **Time: 22 minutes**   🎩 **Serve: 4**

Nutritional Value

(Amount per Serving):

Calories 149
Fat 4 g
Carbohydrates 22 g
Sugar 0 g
Protein 5 g
Cholesterol 0 mg

Ingredients:

- 14 oz can chickpeas, rinsed, drained and pat dry
- 1/2 tsp chili powder
- 1 tbsp olive oil
- Pepper
- Salt

Directions:

1. Place the air fryer Basket onto the Baking Pan and spray air fryer basket with cooking spray.
2. Add chickpeas, chili powder, oil, pepper, and salt into the bowl and toss well.
3. Spread chickpeas on air fryer basket.
4. Place assembled baking pan into Rack Position 2.
5. Set to air fry at 375°F for 12 minutes.
6. Serve and enjoy.

Parmesan Brussels sprouts

⊕ **Time: 22 minutes**　　🔔 **Serve: 4**

Nutritional Value

(Amount per Serving):

Calories 97
Fat 5 g
Carbohydrates 10 g
Sugar 2 g
Protein 5 g
Cholesterol 4 mg

Ingredients:

- 1 lb Brussels sprouts, cut stems and halved
- 1 tbsp olive oil
- 1/4 cup parmesan cheese, grated
- Pepper
- Salt

1. Place the air fryer Basket onto the Baking Pan and spray air fryer basket with cooking spray.
2. Toss Brussels sprouts, oil, pepper, and salt into the bowl.
3. Transfer Brussels sprouts into the air fryer basket.
4. Place assembled baking pan into Rack Position 2.
5. Set to air fry at 350°F for 12 minutes.
6. Sprinkle with parmesan cheese and serve.

Directions:

Crispy Cauliflower Florets

 Time: 30 minutes   Serve: 4

Nutritional Value

(Amount per Serving):

Calories 160
Fat 14 g
Carbohydrates 8 g
Sugar 3 g
Protein 3 g
Cholesterol 0 mg

Ingredients:

- 5 cups cauliflower florets
- 4 tablespoons olive oil
- 1/2 tsp cumin powder
- 6 garlic cloves, chopped
- 1/2 tsp salt

Directions:

1. Place the air fryer Basket onto the Baking Pan and spray air fryer basket with cooking spray.
2. Add all ingredients into the large bowl and toss well.
3. Add cauliflower florets into the air fryer basket.
4. Place assembled baking pan into Rack Position 2.
5. Set to air fry at 400°F for 20 minutes.
6. Serve and enjoy.

Air Fried Walnuts

 Time: 15 minutes   Serve: 6

Nutritional Value

(Amount per Serving):

Calories 265
Fat 25 g
Carbohydrates 4 g
Sugar 0.5 g
Protein 10 g
Cholesterol 0 mg

Ingredients:

- 2 cups walnuts
- 1 tsp olive oil
- 1/4 tsp chili powder
- Pepper
- Salt

1. Place the air fryer Basket onto the Baking Pan and spray air fryer basket with cooking spray.
2. Add walnuts, chili powder, oil, pepper, and salt into the bowl and toss well.
3. Add walnuts into the air fryer basket.
4. Place assembled baking pan into Rack Position 2.
5. Set to air fry at 350°F for 5 minutes.
6. Serve and enjoy.

Directions:

Jalapeno Poppers

⊕ **Time: 17 minutes**   🧢 **Serve: 10**

Nutritional Value

(Amount per Serving):

Calories 71
Fat 6 g
Carbohydrates 2 g
Sugar 0.6 g
Protein 2 g
Cholesterol 18 mg

Ingredients:

- 10 jalapeno peppers, cut in half, remove seeds & membranes
- 1 tsp garlic powder
- 1/2 cup cheddar cheese, shredded
- 4 oz cream cheese
- 1/4 tsp paprika
- 1/2 tsp chili powder
- 1 tsp ground cumin
- 1 tsp salt

Directions:

1. Place the air fryer Basket onto the Baking Pan and spray air fryer basket with cooking spray.
2. In a small bowl, mix together cream cheese, cheddar cheese, garlic powder, cumin, chili powder, paprika, and salt.
3. Stuff cream cheese mixture into each jalapeno half.
4. Place stuffed jalapeno peppers into the air fryer basket.
5. Place assembled baking pan into Rack Position 2.
6. Set to air fry at 350°F for 7 minutes.
7. Serve and enjoy.

Spicy Cauliflower Florets

⊕ **Time: 15 minutes**   🎩 **Serve: 5**

Nutritional Value

(Amount per Serving):

Calories 104
Fat 8 g
Carbohydrates 6 g
Sugar 2 g
Protein 2 g
Cholesterol 0 mg

Ingredients:

- 1 medium cauliflower head, cut into florets
- 1 tbsp garlic, minced
- 3 tbsp olive oil
- 1/2 tsp old bay seasoning
- 1/4 tsp paprika
- Pepper
- Salt

Directions:

1. Place the air fryer Basket onto the Baking Pan and spray air fryer basket with cooking spray.
2. In a bowl, toss cauliflower with remaining ingredients.
3. Add cauliflower florets into the air fryer basket.
4. Place assembled baking pan into Rack Position 2.
5. Set to air fry at 400°F for 15 minutes.
6. Serve and enjoy.

Baked Cheese Dip

 Time: 35 minutes   Serve: 12

Nutritional Value

(Amount per Serving):

Calories 112
Fat 9 g
Carbohydrates 3 g
Sugar 1 g
Protein 4 g
Cholesterol 24 mg

Ingredients:

- 4 oz cream cheese, cubed
- 1 1/2 cups cheddar cheese, shredded
- 1/2 cup mayonnaise
- 1 small onion, diced
- 1 1/2 cups mozzarella cheese, shredded

Directions:

1. Fit the oven with the rack in position 1. Grease 8-inch baking dish and set aside.
2. Add all ingredients into the mixing bowl and mix until well combined. Pour mixture into the prepared baking dish.
3. Set to bake at 400 for 30 minutes, place the baking dish in the oven.
4. Serve and enjoy.

Onion Dip

⏲ **Time: 50 minutes**   🎓 **Serve: 8**

Nutritional Value

(Amount per Serving):

Calories 325
Fat 25 g
Carbohydrates 14 g
Sugar 4 g
Protein 10 g
Cholesterol 47 mg

Ingredients:

- 1 1/2 onions, chopped
- 1 cup mozzarella cheese, shredded
- 1 cup cheddar cheese, shredded
- 1 1/2 cup mayonnaise
- 1/2 tsp garlic powder
- 1 1/2 cup Swiss cheese, shredded
- Pepper
- Salt

Directions:

1. Fit the oven with the rack in position 1. Grease 8-inch baking dish and set aside.
2. Add all ingredients into the mixing bowl and mix until well combined. Pour mixture into the prepared baking dish.
3. Set to bake at 350 for 40 minutes, place the baking dish in the oven.
4. Serve and enjoy.

Delicious Ricotta Dip

 Time: 25 minutes   Serve: 6

Nutritional Value

(Amount per Serving):

Calories 120
Fat 9 g
Carbohydrates 3 g
Sugar 0.2 g
Protein 6 g
Cholesterol 17 mg

Ingredients:

- 1/4 cup parmesan cheese, grated
- 1/2 cup mozzarella cheese, shredded
- 1 tbsp rosemary, chopped
- 1 cup ricotta cheese, shredded
- 1 tbsp lemon juice
- 2 tbsp olive oil
- 2 garlic cloves, minced
- Pepper
- Salt

Directions:

1. Fit the oven with the rack in position 1. Grease baking dish and set aside.
2. Add all ingredients into the mixing bowl and mix until well combined.
3. Pour mixture into the prepared baking dish.
4. Set to bake at 400 F for 15 minutes, place the baking dish in the oven.
5. Serve and enjoy.

Garlic Cheese Dip

 Time: 30 minutes    Serve: 12

Nutritional Value

(Amount per Serving):

Calories 157
Fat 14 g
Carbohydrates 1 g
Sugar 0.1 g
Protein 6 g
Cholesterol 41 mg

Ingredients:

- 3 garlic cloves, minced
- 1 cup mozzarella cheese, shredded
- 8 oz cream cheese, softened
- 5 oz Asiago cheese, shredded
- 1 cup sour cream

Directions:

1. Fit the oven with the rack in position 1. Grease baking dish and set aside.
2. Add all ingredients into the mixing bowl and mix until well combined.
3. Pour mixture into the prepared baking dish.
4. Set to bake at 350 F for 20 minutes, place the baking dish in the oven.
5. Serve and enjoy.

Spinach Dip

 Time: 30 minutes   Serve: 12

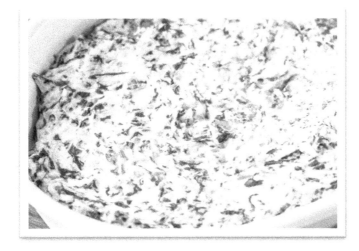

Nutritional Value

(Amount per Serving):

Calories 185
Fat 10 g
Carbohydrates 2 g
Sugar 0.5 g
Protein 7 g
Cholesterol 49 mg

Ingredients:

- 3 oz frozen spinach, defrosted & chopped
- 2 cups cheddar cheese, shredded
- 8 oz cream cheese
- 1 cup sour cream
- 1 tsp garlic salt

1. Fit the oven with the rack in position 1. Grease baking dish and set aside.
2. Add all ingredients into the mixing bowl and mix until well combined. Transfer mixture into the baking dish.
3. Set to bake at 350 F for 20 minutes, place the baking dish in the oven.
4. Serve and enjoy.

Directions:

Spicy Almonds

 Time: 30 minutes  Serve: 6

Nutritional Value

(Amount per Serving):

Calories 117
Fat 16 g
Carbohydrates 6 g
Sugar 1 g
Protein 5 g
Cholesterol 10 mg

Ingredients:

- 1 1/2 cups raw almonds
- 1/2 tsp garlic powder
- 1/2 tsp cumin
- 1 1/2 tsp chili powder
- 2 tsp Worcestershire sauce
- 1/2 tsp cayenne
- 1/4 tsp onion powder
- 1/4 tsp dried basil
- 2 tbsp butter, melted
- 1/2 tsp sea salt

Directions:

1. Line the Baking Pan with foil and set aside.
2. In a mixing bowl, whisk together butter, Worcestershire sauce, chili powder, cumin, garlic powder, basil, onion powder, cayenne, and salt.
3. Add almonds and toss to coat.
4. Spread almonds onto the prepared baking pan.
5. Place the baking pan into rack position 2.
6. Set to Convection Bake at 350°F for 20 minutes.
7. Serve and enjoy.

Spicy Brussels sprouts

 Time: 45 minutes   Serve: 6

Nutritional Value

(Amount per Serving):

Calories 85
Fat 8 g
Carbohydrates 3 g
Sugar 0.7 g
Protein 1 g
Cholesterol 0 mg

Ingredients:

- 2 cups Brussels sprouts, halved
- 1/4 tsp cayenne pepper
- 1/4 tsp garlic powder
- 1/4 cup olive oil
- 1/4 tsp salt

Directions:

1. Line the Baking Pan with foil and set aside.
2. Add all ingredients into the large bowl and toss well.
3. Transfer Brussels sprouts on a baking pan.
4. Place the baking pan into rack position 2.
5. Set to Convection Bake at 400°F for 35 minutes.
6. Serve and enjoy.

Herb Mushrooms

 Time: 24 minutes   **Serve: 4**

Nutritional Value

(Amount per Serving):

Calories 27
Fat 0.4 g
Carbohydrates 4 g
Sugar 2 g
Protein 3 g
Cholesterol 0 mg

Ingredients:

- 1 lb mushrooms
- 1 tbsp basil, minced
- 1 garlic clove, minced
- 1/2 tbsp vinegar
- 1/2 tsp ground coriander
- 1 tsp rosemary, chopped
- Pepper
- Salt

Directions:

1. Place the air fryer Basket onto the Baking Pan and spray air fryer basket with cooking spray.
2. Add all ingredients into the large bowl and toss well.
3. Spread mushrooms onto the baking pan.
4. Place assembled baking pan into Rack Position 2.
5. Set to air fry at 350°F for 14 minutes.
6. Serve and enjoy.

DESSERTS

Banana Butter Brownie

 Time: 26 minutes   Serve: 4

Nutritional Value

(Amount per Serving):

Calories 80
Fat 2 g
Carbohydrates 11 g
Protein 7 g
Sugars 5 g
Cholesterol 15 mg

Ingredients:

- 1 cup bananas, overripe
- 1 scoop protein powder
- 2 tbsp cocoa powder
- 1/2 cup almond butter, melted

Directions:

1. Fit the oven with the rack in position 1. Grease baking dish and set aside.
2. Add all ingredients into the blender and blend until smooth.
3. Pour batter into the prepared baking dish.
4. Set to bake at 350 for 16 minutes, place the baking dish in the oven.
5. Serve and enjoy.

Apple Bars

🕐 **Time: 55 minutes** 🎩 **Serve: 8**

Nutritional Value

(Amount per Serving):

Calories 160
Fat 15 g
Carbohydrates 6 g
Sugar 2 g
Protein 2 g
Cholesterol 0 mg

Ingredients:

- 1/4 cup dried apples
- 1 1/2 tsp baking powder
- 1 1/2 tsp cinnamon
- 1 tbsp ground flax seed
- 1/4 cup coconut butter, softened
- 1 cup pecans
- 1 cup of water
- 1 tsp vanilla
- 2 tbsp swerve

Directions:

1. Fit the oven with the rack in position 1. Grease 8*inch baking dish and set aside.
2. Add all ingredients into the blender and blend until smooth.
3. Pour blended mixture into the prepared dish.
4. Set to bake at 350 for 45 minutes, place the baking dish in the oven.
5. Slice and serve.

Butter Cake

 **Time: 40 minutes**    **Serve: 8**

Nutritional Value

(Amount per Serving):

Calories 211
Fat 11 g
Carbohydrates 27 g
Sugar 16 g
Protein 2 g
Cholesterol 45 mg

Ingredients:

- 1 egg, beaten
- 1 cup all-purpose flour
- 1/2 cup butter, softened
- 1/2 tsp vanilla
- 3/4 cup sugar

Directions:

1. Fit the oven with the rack in position 1. Grease 8*inch baking dish and set aside.
2. In a mixing bowl, mix together sugar and butter.
3. Add egg, flour, and vanilla and mix until combined.
4. Pour batter into the prepared baking dish.
5. Set to bake at 350 for 30 minutes, place the baking dish in the oven.
6. Slice and serve.

Cinnamon Cranberry Muffins

⊕ Time: 40 minutes   🧢 Serve: 6

Nutritional Value

(Amount per Serving):

Calories 218
Fat 16 g
Carbohydrates 18 g
Sugar 10 g
Protein 8 g
Cholesterol 59 mg

Ingredients:

- 2 eggs
- 1 tsp baking powder
- 1/4 cup Swerve
- 1 1/2 cups almond flour
- 1 tsp vanilla
- 1/4 cup sour cream
- 1/2 cup cranberries
- 1/4 tsp cinnamon
- Pinch of salt

Directions:

1. Fit the oven with the rack in position 1. Line 6-cup muffin pan with cupcake liners and set aside.
2. In a bowl, beat sour cream, vanilla, and eggs. Add remaining ingredients except for cranberries and beat until smooth.
3. Add cranberries and fold well.
4. Pour batter into the prepared muffin pan.
5. Set to bake at 325 F for 30 minutes, place the muffin pan in the oven.
6. Serve and enjoy.

Delicious Apple Cake

 Time: 55 minutes   Serve: 12

Nutritional Value

(Amount per Serving):

Calories 200
Fat 4 g
Carbohydrates 38 g
Sugar 11 g
Protein 3 g
Cholesterol 10 mg

Ingredients:

- 2 cups apples, peeled and chopped
- 3 cups all-purpose flour
- 3 tsp baking powder
- 1 1/2 tbsp ground cinnamon
- 1/4 cup sugar
- 1/4 cup butter, melted
- 12 oz unsweetened apple juice
- 1 tsp Salt

1. Fit the oven with the rack in position 1. Grease 8-inch baking dish and set aside.
2. In a large bowl, mix together flour, salt, sugar, cinnamon, and baking powder.
3. Add melted butter and apple juice and mix until well combined.
4. Add apples and fold well.
5. Pour batter into the prepared baking dish.
6. Set to bake at 350 F for 45 minutes, place the baking dish in the oven.
7. Serve and enjoy.

Directions:

Apple Crisp

⊕ Time: 45 minutes   🥘 Serve: 4

Nutritional Value

(Amount per Serving):

Calories 450
Fat 21 g
Carbohydrates 65 g
Sugar 40 g
Protein 4 g
Cholesterol 0 mg

Ingredients:

- 4 1/2 cups apples, diced
- 1 tsp ground cinnamon
- 1 tbsp cornstarch
- 1 tsp vanilla
- 1/2 lemon juice
- 1/8 tsp ground clove
- 1/8 tsp ground nutmeg
- 2 tbsp honey
- For topping:
- 1/3 cup honey
- 1/2 cup almond flour
- 1 cup rolled oats
- 1/3 cup coconut oil, melted
- 1 tsp cinnamon

Directions:

1. Fit the oven with the rack in position 1. Grease 7-inch baking dish and set aside.
2. In a medium bowl, mix apples, vanilla, lemon juice, and honey. Sprinkle spices and cornstarch on top and stir well.
3. Pour apple mixture into the prepared baking dish.
4. In a small bowl, mix together coconut oil, cinnamon, almond

flour, oats, and honey and spread on top of apple mixture.

5. Set to bake at 350 F for 35 minutes, place the baking dish in the oven.
6. Serve and enjoy.

Easy Mini Chocolate Cake

 Time: 40 minutes Serve: 4

Nutritional Value

(Amount per Serving):

Calories 385

Fat 24 g

Carbohydrates 41 g

Sugar 25 g

Protein 5 g

Cholesterol 49 mg

Ingredients:

- 1 egg
- 1/2 cup all-purpose flour
- 1/3 cup sour cream
- 1/2 cup granulated sugar
- 1/3 cup canola oil
- 1/2 tsp baking soda
- 1 tbsp warm coffee
- 1/2 tsp vanilla
- 5 tbsp cocoa powder

Directions:

1. Fit the oven with the rack in position 1. Grease 6-inch baking dish and set aside.
2. In a medium bowl, whisk together flour, baking soda, and cocoa powder and set aside.
3. In a small bowl, whisk together egg, vanilla, coffee, sour cream, sugar, and oil.
4. Pour egg mixture into the flour mixture and mix until just combined.
5. Pour batter into the prepared baking dish.
6. Set to bake at 350 F for 30 minutes, place the baking dish in the oven.
7. Serve and enjoy.

Almond Raspberry Muffins

 Time: 45 minutes   Serve: 6

Nutritional Value

(Amount per Serving):

Calories 227
Fat 18 g
Carbohydrates 13 g
Sugar 7 g
Protein 7 g
Cholesterol 55 mg

Ingredients:

- 2 eggs
- 3.5 oz raspberries
- 1 tsp baking powder
- 5 oz almond meal
- 2 tbsp coconut oil
- 2 tbsp honey

Directions:

1. Fit the oven with the rack in position 1. Line 6-cup muffin pan with cupcake liners and set aside.
2. In a medium bowl, mix together almond meal and baking powder.
3. Add honey, eggs, and oil and stir until just combined. Add raspberries and fold well.
4. Spoon batter into the six silicone muffin molds.
5. Set to bake at 350 F for 35 minutes, place the muffin pan in the oven.
6. Serve and enjoy.

Tasty Baked Apples

 Time: 50 minutes   Serve: 4

Nutritional Value

(Amount per Serving):

Calories 274
Fat 12 g
Carbohydrates 45 g
Sugar 35 g
Protein 1 g
Cholesterol 31 mg

Ingredients:

- 4 apples, peeled, cored, and cut into 1/2-inch chunks
- 1 tbsp ground cinnamon
- 2 tbsp fresh lemon juice
- 1/3 cup brown sugar
- 1/4 cup butter, cubed
- 1 tsp cornstarch
- 1/2 tsp nutmeg

Directions:

1. Fit the oven with the rack in position 1. Grease 6-inch baking dish and set aside.
2. Add all ingredients into the bowl and mix until just combined.
3. Pour apple mixture into the prepared baking dish. Cover dish with foil.
4. Set to bake at 400 F for 40 minutes, place the baking dish in the oven.
5. Serve and enjoy.

Cinnamon Baked Peaches

Time: 40 minutes   Serve: 4

Nutritional Value

(Amount per Serving):

Calories 199
Fat 12 g
Carbohydrates 25 g
Sugar 22 g
Protein 1 g
Cholesterol 31 mg

Ingredients:

- 4 freestone peaches, cut in half and remove stones
- 1 tsp cinnamon
- 4 tbsp butter, cut into pieces
- 2 tbsp sugar
- 8 tsp brown sugar

Directions:

1. Fit the oven with the rack in position 1. Grease baking dish and set aside.
2. Place peach halves in a baking dish and fill each half with 1 tsp brown sugar.
3. Place butter pieces on top of each peach halves.
4. Mix together cinnamon and sugar and sprinkle over peaches.
5. Set to bake at 375 F for 30 minutes, place the baking dish in the oven.
6. Serve and enjoy.

Healthy Carrot Cake

 Time: 35 minutes 　　 Serve: 4

Nutritional Value

(Amount per Serving):

Calories 341
Fat 20 g
Carbohydrates 40 g
Sugar 25 g
Protein 5 g
Cholesterol 41 mg

Ingredients:

- 1 egg
- 1/4 cup grated carrot
- 1/2 tsp vanilla
- 1/2 tsp cinnamon
- 1/2 cup sugar
- 1/4 cup canola oil
- 1/4 cup walnuts, chopped
- 1/2 tsp baking powder
- 1/2 cup flour

Directions:

1. Fit the oven with the rack in position 1. Grease 6-inch baking dish and set aside.
2. In a medium bowl, beat sugar and oil for 1 minute. Add vanilla, cinnamon, and egg and beat for 30 seconds.
3. Add remaining ingredients and stir everything well until just combined.
4. Pour batter into the prepared baking dish.
5. Set to bake at 350 F for 25 minutes, place the baking dish in the oven.
6. Serve and enjoy.

Cinnamon Carrot Muffins

 Time: 30 minutes 　　 Serve: 6

Nutritional Value

(Amount per Serving):

Calories 165
Fat 2 g
Carbohydrates 33 g
Sugar 16 g
Protein 3 g
Cholesterol 27 mg

Ingredients:

- 1 egg
- 1 cup all-purpose flour
- 3/4 cup grated carrots
- 1 tsp vanilla
- 1/4 cup light brown sugar
- 1/4 cup granulated sugar
- 1/2 tbsp canola oil
- 1 1/2 tsp baking powder
- 1/4 tsp nutmeg
- 1 tsp cinnamon
- 1/4 cup applesauce
- 1/4 tsp salt

Directions:

1. Fit the oven with the rack in position 1. Line 6-cup muffin pan with cupcake liners and set aside.
2. Add all ingredients into the bowl and mix until well combined.
3. Pour batter into prepared muffin pan.
4. Set to bake at 350 F for 20 minutes, place the muffin pan in the oven.
5. Serve and enjoy.

Tasty Lemon Cupcakes

 Time: 25 minutes 　　 Serve: 6

Nutritional Value

(Amount per Serving):

Calories 200
Fat 6 g
Carbohydrates 34 g
Sugar 17 g
Protein 3 g
Cholesterol 29 mg

Ingredients:

- 1 egg
- 1 tsp lemon zest, grated
- 1/2 cup sugar
- 1 cup flour
- 1/2 tsp vanilla
- 1/2 cup milk
- 2 tbsp canola oil
- 1/4 tsp baking soda
- 3/4 tsp baking powder
- 1/2 tsp salt

Directions:

1. Fit the oven with the rack in position 1. Line 6-cup muffin pan with cupcake liners and set aside.
2. In a bowl, whisk egg, vanilla, milk, oil, and sugar until creamy.
3. Add remaining ingredients and stir until just combined.
4. Pour batter into the prepared muffin pan.
5. Set to bake at 350 F for 15 minutes, place the muffin pan in the oven.
6. Serve and enjoy.

Brownie Muffins

🕐 Time: 25 minutes 🧢 Serve: 6

Nutritional Value

(Amount per Serving):

Calories 164
Fat 15 g
Carbohydrates 4 g
Sugar 0.5 g
Protein 6 g
Cholesterol 110 mg

Ingredients:

- 3 eggs
- 1 cup almond flour
- 1 tbsp gelatin
- 1/3 cup butter, melted
- 1/3 cup cocoa powder
- 1/2 cup Swerve

Directions:

1. Fit the oven with the rack in position 1. Line 6-cup muffin pan with cupcake liners and set aside.
2. Add all ingredients into the bowl and stir until just combined.
3. Pour batter into the prepared muffin pan.
4. Set to bake at 350 F for 15 minutes, place the muffin pan in the oven.
5. Serve and enjoy.

Delicious Scalloped Pineapple

⊕ **Time: 45 minutes**   🍮 **Serve: 6**

Nutritional Value

(Amount per Serving):

Calories 509
Fat 17.8 g
Carbohydrates 85.7 g
Sugar 71.1 g
Protein 3.4 g
Cholesterol 123 mg

Ingredients:

- 3 eggs, lightly beaten
- 4 cups of bread cubes
- ¼ cup milk
- ½ cup butter, melted
- 8 oz can crushed pineapple, un-drained
- 2 cups of sugar

Directions:

1. Fit the oven with the rack in position 1. Grease 8-inch baking dish and set aside.
2. In a mixing bowl, whisk eggs with milk, butter, crushed pineapple, and sugar. Add bread cubes and stir well to coat.
3. Transfer mixture to the prepared baking dish. Set to bake at 350 F for about 35 minutes. After 5 minutes, transfer the baking dish to the oven.
4. Once done, let it cool for 10 minutes.
5. Serve and enjoy.

CPSIA information can be obtained
at www.ICGtesting.com
Printed in the USA
LVHW011918291020
670161LV00004B/291